NEXT STEPS

A Practical Guide to Planning for
the Best Half of Your Life

NEXT STEPS

A Practical Guide to Planning for the Best Half of Your Life

by Jan Warner and Jan Collins

Fresno, California

Next Steps® is distributed by United Feature Syndicate, Inc. and
Newspaper Enterprise Association, Inc. www.unitedfeatures.com

Published by Quill Driver Books
an imprint of Linden Publishing
2006 South Mary, Fresno, California 93721
559-233-6633 / 800-345-4447
QuillDriverBooks.com

Quill Driver Books and Colophon are trademarks of
Linden Publishing, Inc.

Quill Driver Books project cadre:
Doris Hall, John David Marion, Stephen Blake Mettee,
Kent Sorsky, Maura J. Zimmer

ISBN 978-1-884956-96-6 (1-884956-96-3)

135798642

Printed in the United States of America
on acid-free paper.

Library of Congress Cataloging-in-Publication Data

Warner, Jan, 1942-
  Next steps : a practical guide to planning for the best half of your life /
by Jan Warner and Jan Collins.
     p. cm.
  Includes index.
  ISBN-13: 978-1-884956-96-6 (pbk. : alk. paper)
  ISBN-10: 1-884956-96-3 (pbk. : alk. paper)
  1. Retirement--Planning. 2. Portfolio management. I. Collins, Jan. II.
Title.
  HQ1062.W374 2009
  646.7'9--dc22
                              2009010315

Acknowledgments

We thank our readers for helping us understand the issues that face them. We also thank Westlaw for providing legal research, and United Media for distributing these important columns to the public, both via newspapers and electronically. And we thank Jan Warner's partners, Charles M. Black, Jr. and Mitchell C. Payne of the law firm Warner, Payne and Black, LLP.

—Jan Warner and Jan Collins

To our indomitable, octogenarian mothers—
Naomi Warner and Gerry Collins.

Contents

Prologue

For several reasons, those of us who were raised in the 1950s and 1960s didn't see assisted-living facilities, nursing homes, and senior retirement communities proliferating in our communities.

First, life expectancy was much lower than it is today, meaning that only a small percentage of the population lived into their 70s, 80s and 90s.

Second, when Mom, Dad, or Aunt Emma suffered a debilitating stroke or had memory lapses (now called dementia), these relatives were usually cared for at home by family members. (In those days, most families were sustained by a single wage earner.)

Third, if it was impossible to provide care at home, there were some small nursing facilities or, in some instances, a caregiver who would open her home and care for one or two disabled adults. Jan Warner remembers that after his grandmother's stroke in the late 1960s, she stayed with a caregiver at a cost of $150 per week because both of her daughters worked outside the home.

Things are different today, with longer life expectancies, more elderly people on fixed incomes, more two-wage-earner families, a much higher cost of care, and an uncertain economy.

Having practiced law for nearly 41 years, Jan Warner has seen first hand the significant issues that face elderly people and their families. In fact, his firm was practicing "elder law" before it had a name—and he didn't even know it.

In 1989, we began coauthoring FlyingSolo®, a newspaper column about divorce and separation that was initially syndicated by Knight-Ridder and now by United Media. Seeing the increasing number of reader questions about how to deal with issues affecting the elderly and the disabled, in 1998 we began coauthoring NextSteps®, a newspaper column about these topics that is also syndicated by United Media.

This book is the product of our columns, reader questions from throughout the country, and more than four decades of experience regarding what folks need to do to avoid making bad decisions, avoid paying lawyers to fix the fixable ones, and avoid costly family disputes.

—*Jan Warner and Jan Collins*

Introduction

Certainty? "In this world, nothing is certain but death and taxes," Benjamin Franklin said back in 1789. While this advice remains sound more than two centuries later, the vast majority of seniors and seniors-to-be (i.e., the millions of Baby Boomers) today are experiencing, or will experience, "certainties" that our Founding Fathers never contemplated.

In Ben Franklin's day, few Americans lived into their 80s and beyond. Today, people in their 80s are the fastest-growing segment of the U.S. population, and many may well outlive their retirements and die penniless after long illnesses. And those who escape long-term illnesses may leave the "well spouse" without sufficient resources to subsist due to economics.

Many of these individuals will require institutionalization at considerable cost, causing the wealth that once passed from generation to generation to decrease significantly. Indeed, not even 1 percent of Americans who die each year will have estates large enough to require payments of estate taxes. The rest will leave behind precious little to pass on to their children and grandchildren.

Today's "Sandwich Generation" family is being emotionally and financially crunched. These are the folks taking care of aging family members, juggling two jobs in order to pay current household bills, and trying to educate their children while also attempting to save enough for their own retirements and possible long-term care needs. Divorce, remarriage, second families, and cohabitation later in life are also part of the 21st-century mix that complicates what were once called the "Golden Years."

So, instead of concerning ourselves with estate taxes at death, which more than 99 percent of us will not pay, the overwhelming majority of us should instead 1) recognize what can happen to us and our families during our lifetimes, and then 2) develop a written life plan that allows trusted family members or others to implement our plan should we, our spouses, or significant others become chronically ill or incapacitated—that is, unable to take care of ourselves because of cognitive or physical problems. Alzheimer's disease, dementia, and other cognitive maladies are striking more and younger Americans, placing families in untenable positions of paying for care or stopping work to provide needed care. Likewise, stroke, multiple sclerosis, muscular dystrophy, and Lou Gehrig's disease are disrupting the enjoyment of retirement and the efforts at continued family planning.

The truth is that none of us knows whether we will remain healthy into our old age. Anyone can develop physical or mental conditions that require long-term care. If we are unprepared, we could lose everything and become dependent upon the social welfare system. And if there is a spouse, he or she will become dependent on adult children who may already be swimming in debt.

There is an additional factor to consider: Since seniors and seniors-to-be cumulatively hold a significant portion of the wealth in this country, they are often targets for scams and bad advice.

Next Steps: A Practical Guide to Planning for the Best Half of Your Life will help you understand the issues and risks that you and your family face, choose the professionals who can help, and develop a plan that will be sufficiently flexible to maximize your options and stand the test of time. We all want to control our own destinies. *Next Steps* shows you how to do so, step-by-step.

So, what is the *Next Steps* plan? Simply put, it is the recruitment and development of a team of professionals who can help seniors and Boomers alike prepare a series of documents tailored to your specifications and based on your needs that will: 1) allow maximum flexibility for trusted persons to make financial decisions should you, the signer, become incapacitated and unable to make decisions; 2) provide directions to a trusted person to make your health-care decisions according to your wishes, should you be unable to express your wishes; and 3) ensure that at your death, your remaining assets flow to those whom you intend to receive them.

Why do you need a plan? Because without a plan in place, no one is in charge if you become incapacitated, meaning an over-burdened court system may well make decisions for you without knowing your intentions. Without such a plan, there is also the potential of emotional and physical abuse from family members or caregivers; court-imposed restrictions that would take away the ability to plan; and significant additional expense, given the cost of lawyers and medical professionals. Finally, your assets may well go to the wrong people.

The goal of your life plan is straightforward: to put your directions in writing, clearly and concisely, so that if you become unable to make your decisions because of incapacity, there will be an orderly transfer of authority to trusted persons who will ensure that you and your spouse—or significant other—are properly cared for.

In 1992, there were approximately 32 million Americans over the age of 64. By 2030, that number is expected to swell to more than 70 million. These numbers will create an unprecedented demand on our health-care and long-term-care systems; incapacity is no longer an unlikely occurrence.

Without proper planning, long-term care can decimate an estate, leave the "well spouse" next to penniless, and leave those who might have been heirs out of luck.

Here's what you need to do....

SECTION I:
Choosing Your Team and Making It Work

1

Putting Together the Right Team for You

Why You Need a Team

For the vast majority of us who won't have taxable estates, the planning process should involve not just financial or estate planning, but also life planning, long-term care planning, death planning, burial planning, and even pet planning, if we own animals. Indeed, planning for your future is "not your father's Oldsmobile." Given the billions of dollars Boomers and their parents have lost during the largest downturn in our nation's history—with no idea when it will bottom out—coupled with lost equity in real estate investments, even greater planning challenges face all Americans today.

Times have changed, and so have our priorities. This is true not only for seniors born before 1946, but also for Baby Boomers born between 1946 and 1964. Planning your future is more essential today than ever before given tough economic times (that we don't believe will be getting any better soon), and the ever-increasing financial abuse of seniors by family members and caregivers.

Until now, each preceding generation of Americans was better off economically than their parents because of ample job opportunities, a thriving economy, and appreciable inheritances. Recent times, however, don't bode so well for our progeny. When you couple a frail economy, a schizophrenic stock market, and the "running-on-empty" Social Security and Medicare systems with the rising costs of living, medical care, prescriptions, and long-term care—and then add in the reality of fewer jobs—it's a good bet that Boomers will inherit little, if anything, from their parents. And Boomers' children may get even less.

At the same time, Boomers live much differently than their parents. Many have incurred significant debt and live beyond their means, skip from job to job, and wait for the retirement that may never come. In addition, because they have been marrying and having children later in life, Boomers are still writing checks for children's college educations and incurring debt well into late-middle age and beyond. Plus, divorce and remarriage are further thinning assets and available cash flow.

In today's uncertain economy, company loyalty and, on the opposite end of the spectrum, loyalty to the company, are things of the past. Jobs are being cut by the hundreds of thousands and Boomers are being "put out to pasture" early. Many have lost much of their wealth and retirement stake in the wake of the ongoing stock market gyrations, the demise of a significant part of the banking and investment banking industries, the wave of home foreclosures stemming from the subprime mortgage mess, and an increasing number of sour real estate deals.

Sadly, intra-family deception in America today is increasing, often causing litigation when children have taken advantage of their vulnerable parents. More and more cases are showing up on court dockets where children or other family members, who are ostensibly caring for elderly parents or relatives, keep the frail seniors from communicating with other relatives, abuse powers of attorney, and even hire lawyers to prepare documents for the elderly seniors who, over time, will stick up for the caregiver, not unlike in hostage situations.

Meanwhile, seniors are concerned about how to pass on assets in a manner that won't go up in the smoke of a divorce case, or be put in the hands of a child or grandchild with drug or alcohol problems. As if all this weren't enough, Americans today are seeing their dollars buy less, even as they pay more for gasoline, food, utilities, and health care. Tax cuts seem to have shifted the burden to the middle class.

What all this means is that seniors and Boomers must develop plans for life, for the possibility of incapacity, and for death—in that order. Creating and implementing these plans, and merging them into a master plan, must be a multidisciplinary effort undertaken with the assistance of a qualified team of professionals.

Who Should Be on Your Team

Today's planning requires a *team* of professionals because the legal, economic, and health issues that concern older people are all interrelated. The lawyer who helps you with your plan, for example, may need input from medical, financial, and accounting professionals, not to mention trusted family members.

In the legal arena alone, a senior's planning is impacted in many unique ways by Medicare, Medicaid, Social Security, veterans' benefits, estate planning, marriage and remarriage issues, estate administration, planning for long-term care, nursing home laws and regulations, age discrimination, health-care law, elder abuse and fraud, incapacity (and the planning for it), and retirement benefits.

Therefore, depending on your assets, income, and goals, you will need a lawyer experienced in geriatric issues who will take time to understand your individual needs, develop a plan to fit those needs, and provide you with documents that meet those needs; a certified public accountant to help with the taxation issues should any exist; an experienced geriatric care manager (depending on your situation) to assist should there be the necessity of long-term care placement; possibly a financial advisor or insurance agent who doesn't sell products just to receive commissions; and a physician with experience in geriatrics.

So, how do you find this team of competent professionals? The following sections will lead you through the process:

Finding and Hiring the Right Lawyer

Finding and hiring the right lawyer is probably your most important task because you will be placing your personal and economic future in that person's hands. Whereas "estate planning" is designed to aid in the disposition of your assets after you die, "elder law" is geared toward addressing issues that affect you while you are still living—so that you can decide now what will be done should you become incapacitated.

To begin with, seek out a lawyer who is experienced in and understands the issues facing you and your family. The "old country lawyer" of the 1950s and 1960s who was all things to all people no longer exists. Like the medical profession, there are areas of the law in which lawyers tend to specialize or limit their practices. While comparatively few law schools have a curriculum in the area of elder law, there are competent, experienced lawyers throughout the United States who can handle your plan for you. You don't need a lawyer friend who won't charge you. You don't need a lawyer who prepares "one-size-fits-all" documents and changes only the name of the client on the word processer. And, because of the significant potential of adverse ramifications, we don't believe you should prepare documents yourself from form books or online. Because of the many planning nuances that may affect you—but that you probably don't know about—preparing your own documents is like driving your car blindfolded. You can't afford to try it.

The cost of securing appropriate legal documents is an investment in your own and your family's future. If you are looking for a cheap job, or if you choose to get your documents from the Internet or some other "do-it-yourself" source, you will get what you pay for. No one benefits from being penny-wise and pound-foolish in this business because, should you become incapacitated, you will not be able to change your documents.

Finding a lawyer who understands the nuances of issues affecting you may not be as easy as you think. You certainly can ask friends and family whom they may have used, and find out what they liked—and didn't like—about their lawyer. But we believe the best alternative is for you to come armed with sufficient information so that when you interview a prospective lawyer, you will ask the right questions and properly enlighten him or her about your particular situation. Unless you give the lawyer the entire perspective of your family and what you would like to accomplish, he or she won't be able to help. Remember that the lawyer is the medium, the author who will write your documents to fit *your* needs to comply with both your wishes and the law.

A good starting point in finding this crucial member of your team may be the National Academy of Elder Law Attorneys (**www.naela.org**), where you can search for member attorneys who have knowledge in this area. Just because a lawyer is a member of this organization does not mean he or she will fit the bill for you, however. There is nothing better than a face-to-face interview, so that you can find a sufficient comfort level with the person who will play such a key role on your team.

Finding a Certified Public Accountant

While many seniors don't file tax returns, if, as part of your plan, you are taking distributions from your retirement and IRA and are earning interest and dividends, it may well be that a portion of your Social Security will be subject to income taxes. If you don't already have a Certified Public Accountant (CPA), you may need one to assist you in the planning process, especially if your assets include "qualified" money—such as IRAs and 401(k)s, or low-basis stocks or property that will cause capital gains (and the tax thereon) when you sell them. Any sales transaction that results in a taxable gain should be reviewed by a CPA in order to avoid potential future problems with tax authorities.

Additionally, if there is a family business involved that should be evaluated or appraised, a CPA or, in some instances, a Certified Valuation Analyst (CVA) will be a necessary ingredient. Another reason to engage a CPA who engages in tax preparation and planning for the elderly is that they are also aware of what medical and long-term care expenses can be deducted. If you can't find a Certified Public Accountant, go to **www.aicpa.org**, or check out the membership of your state chapter of the American Institute of Certified Public Accountants.

Finding a Geriatric Care Manager

Professional geriatric care managers are generally nurses or social workers who specialize in dealing with matters affecting the disabled and elderly, especially those who require assistance at home or in facilities. Geriatric care managers are excellent sources of information about levels of care, and they are often used as private patient advocates in the hospital discharge planning process. By level of care, we mean how and where the elderly person will most likely get the type of care required for their condition in the least restrictive environment. They also assess individuals who require assistance, and then help create plans of care within the family budget. They can even help find appropriate facilities and home care agencies for those who need them.

By going to **www.caremanager.org**, you will find a listing of members of the National Association of Professional Geriatric Care Managers near you.

Finding a Financial Advisor

Depending on your financial situation, you may or may not need a financial advisor. Given the recent huge swings in the stock market, whether you remain in the market or stay on the sidelines is clearly your choice. One important thing to remember, however, is that, depending on your age, the accumulation of assets in the future may not be in the cards unless you stand to inherit well or win the lottery. In our view, preservation of principal is essential for seniors because future asset acquisition is unlikely. Additionally, seniors must be careful not to get caught up in the numerous scams that permeate the investment community today.

If you do choose an investment advisor, that person or entity should never serve as your attorney, personal representative, or trustee. We recommend that if you hire a financial advisor, you should consider a "fee only" advisor—that is, an advisor who does not take a fee based on products sold or a percentage of your account. If you choose a trust department of a bank or brokerage as your trustee, we believe there is a conflict of interest for that same entity to manage your investments. So keep your eyes open.

To find a financial advisor, go to **www.adviserinfo.sec.gov/ IAPD/Content/Search/iapd_OrgSearch.aspx**.

And to find out if there have been complaints filed against a potential broker or financial advisor, go to **www.finra.org/Investors/ToolsCalculators/BrokerCheck/index.htm** or **www.sec.gov/investor/brokers.htm**.

Finding a Physician

In our opinion, seniors need doctors with expertise in geriatrics. Yet, despite the ballooning number of seniors, geriatricians are comparatively few and far between. You might check your local Yellow Pages or talk to friends. If you are lucky enough to live in a city or town with a medical school, you can often find geriatric specialists on the faculty.

If no geriatricians are available in your area, internists and family practitioners can certainly provide adequate treatment. Make sure, however, that you have a physician or physician's assistant who will listen to your concerns.

A Few Final Tips

Never appoint a person who is acting as your lawyer, doctor, accountant, or in any other way to also assist you as your agent, trustee, or personal representative.

Never lend money to anyone who is assisting you in the planning process.

Never allow a person or entity acting as your agent, trustee, or personal representative to also manage your investments. In fact, we believe it is a conflict of interest for a bank or brokerage acting as trustee to hold and invest your money in another arm of the same entity.

Your Unique Situation

Once you have found the right people for your team, make sure your lawyer—the lead person on your team—fully understands your unique situation. Everyone is different, and everyone's circumstances are different. What you want is that when your plan is completed, it will serve you through incapacity (if that occurs) without family disputes, and, at your death, what financial resources are left will go where you want them to go—again, without creating family disputes.

Remember, when the different parts of your plan are uncoordinated, litigation is probable, at great financial and emotional costs. Try to cover as many contingencies as possible, in writing, to avoid having a judge or jury who doesn't know what you would have wanted make your decisions for you.

QUESTION: *As far back as I can remember, my parents have been very secretive about their finances. Since my father's death three years ago, my mother, now 82, has allowed a financial advisor whom she met at a seminar for the elderly to handle her finances. He calls her daily and they seem to have a close personal relationship, but I have never met him and she has never offered to introduce us. Now Mom is becoming even more paranoid and secretive about her finances. We have never seen a statement from the financial advisor come to the house in the mail, and she has no other mailing address. Mom's checking account always has a minimum balance each month, and my husband and I are basically supporting her. Is there anything we can do, as we are very concerned?*

ANSWER: The situation you describe is a recipe for disaster—that is, if disaster hasn't already clobbered your mother's investment portfolio. While all individuals are entitled to privacy in their financial dealings, and while we understand your mother's desire to keep these matters private, when elderly persons reach the point that they must depend on family members for their care, it is time for them to be open and to share information just in case the unthinkable—incapacity—occurs. Financial advisors and others in whom elderly persons place their trust should foster and encourage—not discourage and denigrate—family relationships under these circumstances.

TAKING THE NEXTSTEP: Since your mother is not incapacitated, you will not be able to be appointed as her conservator or guardian. We suggest the following: (1) Check out the financial advisor. With whom is he affiliated? Is he a registered investment advisor? Does he hold insurance and/or securities licenses? Has he had complaints lodged against him? Does he have a criminal record? Much of this information is readily available as public information, through the Securities and Exchange Commission (SEC), your state securities agency, and your state insurance commission. (2) Go to the probate or surrogate court where your father's estate was probated and get copies of the estate inventories which will show you what your father owned when he died, his life insurance, etc. These records should give you some ideas about the available funds your mother started with three years ago. (3) Have a heart-to-heart talk with your mother. Tell her about your concerns. Tell her that while you and your husband are certainly willing to continue to help her, you expect her to trust you and, if she does not, then it might be a good idea for you to help her find an assisted-living facility into which she can move. (4) Consider reporting your concerns to your local adult protective services agency, as it appears to us that there is a good probability that your mother, a vulnerable adult, has been taken advantage of by an unscrupulous predator.

2

Working with Your Team

Most of us plan more for a trip to the grocery store than for our lives and deaths. One reason for this is that in today's world, it is often difficult to know whom you can trust. Moreover, life is much more complex than it was even 20 years ago.

Be that as it may, it is essential that you understand the basics of the difficulties you may encounter between now and the time you die, and plan to either avoid or deal with each of them in a way that suits your purposes. This is where your team comes in. They'll help you put together a plan to accomplish your goals. But know that putting your team together is just the first step. Once you have established your team, you must make sure that *you* are in charge of these professionals who are providing services for you. They work for you, and you must empower yourself—via learning all you can—to direct the fashioning of the documents containing your life and death plans.

Seniors face many potential traps and pitfalls. Here are a few important ones for you to be alert to; make sure your team is also entirely aware of them:

Financial Issues

If you have a financial advisor on your team, he or she can help you understand the following issues:

- When seniors go to their local bank to renew a certificate of deposit, they may well be sold a deferred annuity based upon representations from their "account representative" that the annuity will 1) produce greater returns than a new CD (but not that the higher return will be for only six months or a year); 2) defer income taxes (even though most seniors don't have income tax problems and actually need the income); and 3) avoid probate (because an annuity is a non-probate asset that passes according to a beneficiary designation).

  What the senior is also not told is that 1) the bank, as broker in the sale of the annuity, immediately earns a commission of between 3 and 6 percent; 2) if withdrawals of more than 10 percent per year are needed, the senior will be subject to penalties; and 3) if the senior needs the money for health care or other reasons, he or she will be tagged with paying a penalty equal to the commission. Some annuities do not allow surrender for a number of years without penalties.

- Similarly, if you have a brokerage account with an entity—a bank or brokerage firm—and choose that institution to act as your trustee, there are innate conflicts of interest. Even though you may be told that the trust department and investment department are different parts of the bank, they are all under one umbrella. Moving investments from an investment brokerage to a bank brokerage may well result in those holdings being sold and converted into the bank's own private-labeled mutual funds from which the bank earns additional fees. Therefore, in addition to trust and brokerage fees, the bank may well earn fees from their mutual funds, which are difficult to calculate. And, if the bank is also acting as trustee, you are also paying fees for that service. It is not unusual for trust accounts to make little or no money when invested in this fashion, due to the fees. We strongly suggest, therefore, that the person or entity that serves as your trustee or fiduciary not be the same entity that controls your investments.

- Another trap for the unwary: When a broker leaves one employer to go with another and takes his/her clients with him, it is not unusual for the broker to change investments or, where there is an annuity, to utilize what is called a "Section 1035 exchange" to take the cash in an older annuity and "roll it over" tax-free into a new annuity. This action, in turn, starts the clock ticking all over again with regard to the penalty period because the broker has earned yet another commission.

Finally, because there may be taxation issues regarding annuities, life insurance, and financial products, we recommend that seniors utilize the services of a Certified Public Accountant before engaging in any type of financial transaction that could impact this area.

Legal Issues

How you work with the lawyer on your team is of the utmost importance. Please keep in mind this very important point: Conflicts of interest are widespread in every planning area, even when dealing with your lawyer. If you and your spouse seek estate planning advice and document preparation from the same lawyer, for example, that lawyer has conflicts of interest in representing both of you.

So, remember that if a husband and wife go to one lawyer to prepare their estate plans, in order for the lawyer to represent both of them, he is obligated to explain to both parties that he has inherent conflicts of interest, and he must provide a written waiver to be signed by spouses before he begins representation. This is especially important where, as with second marriages, one spouse agrees to waive his/her interest in the other's estate and give up rights that he/she would otherwise have in the other's estate. So, while it is perfectly fine to use one attorney, a husband and wife should always be given an explanation by the attorney of potential conflicts.

Therefore, before that attorney can represent both of you in the estate and life planning arena, both you and your spouse must sign an informed waiver after the lawyer provides you a full disclosure of the potential conflicts and risks of joint representation. This action is necessary so that both of you can make informed decisions regarding the representation. Know also that under attorneys' ethical rules, differences of opinion about the disposition of property could prevent the lawyer from representing both of you without an informed waiver. You should each review that waiver, using separate, independent counsel, in order to avoid the possibility that advice to one of you may influence representation of the other.

Remember, though, that even with an informed waiver, one attorney can't represent both of you in a premarital agreement, a divorce, or a waiver of claims to the other's estate. And, in our opinion, you should never appoint a lawyer as your trustee, personal representative, or other fiduciary.

- Another tip: Do not allow non-lawyers to prepare legal documents for you. In more instances than we like to see, insurance agents and some financial planners sell seniors insurance, annuities, and financial products they don't need. In order to retain control of the relationship or for other reasons, such as earning fees for acting as a fiduciary, some of these non-lawyers offer to save seniors attorney's fees by preparing their wills and powers of attorney, sometimes naming themselves as agents or personal representatives. This is very dangerous.

The unauthorized practice of law occurs when a non-lawyer prepares legal documents and gives advice, consultation, explanation, and recommendations on legal matters. The purpose of barring the unauthorized practice of law is to protect the public from incompetent preparation of legal documents and to prevent harm resulting from inaccurate legal advice. Therefore, even if a non-lawyer fills in blanks for you in a legal software product, the choices of what to include and what not to include may well constitute unauthorized legal aid.

Medical Issues

There are potential issues with your doctor, as well. Here's an example:

Mary goes to the doctor because her medication is making her confused and feel poorly. The doctor, or her assistant, may enter into the chart that Mary is confused, and she may include the word "dementia" or "possible dementia." The problem starts when Mary sees another physician, who sees the first physician's records, and then the word "dementia" finds its way into the second physician's file, and so on. This is called "diagnostic momentum," an offhand reference by a physician in the patient's chart that can lead each succeeding physician to utilize the word "dementia," thus creating a momentum that could well cause Mary problems later when she signs powers of attorney, wills, or trusts.

In point of fact, many "diagnoses" of dementia are, in fact, actually only depression or the combination of medications that potentiate each other. Often, it is not until a person is hospitalized that the true cause of short-term memory loss comes to light. For this reason, it is important that seniors keep watch on their medical records, to which they are entitled copies. While the physician may not be doing anything maliciously, he or she may well be creating difficulties. Therefore, make sure you read your medical record and question the documentation. If you see the word "dementia" and there is nothing to support it, have it excised from the physician's record. Don't be bashful about asking for, and reviewing, your medical records.

issues of hospital discharge placement, capac-
or those unable to perform activities of daily life, we
recommend the use of professional geriatric care managers.
These professionals serve as an interface between the senior and the medical community and are charged with protecting the interests of the senior, not the facility. For example:

> If you have been hospitalized and your Medicare or insurance coverage is coming to an end, the hospital social workers will be looking to make discharge plans to another facility should you require rehabilitation. The hospital discharge planner has the hospital's interest at heart, not yours; therefore, you need an advocate to make sure you are placed in a facility that will be best for you. This is where the geriatric care manager is essential. Since discharge planning should begin at the same time as the hospitalization, we recommend that a geriatric care manager be retained as quickly after hospitalization as possible to assist in the discharge process. To find a geriatric care manager in your area, you can visit **www.caremanager.org**.

Most people spend very little time dealing with their life and death plans, either because they don't feel comfortable dealing with the issues or because they don't understand the importance of making such decisions. Others believe they are healthy and don't need to plan. But knowledge is power, and you must empower yourself to deal with life and death issues by seeking out information and understanding your options. To repeat, *you* must be in charge of, and control, your relationships with the professionals who provide services for you.

One last note: Once your planning documents are prepared, you should update them only if there are significant changes in your life that require modification of your documents. If, for example, you and your spouse have properly prepared documents and one of you dies, there should be no need to re-do your documents so long as 1) you have named in your will alternate beneficiaries and personal representative should your spouse predecease you; 2) you have chosen alternate agents in your power of attorney to act for you in handling finances should you become incapacitated; and 3) you have chosen alternate agents to make your health-care decisions should you become incapacitated.

If, however, you remarry, change your mind about beneficiaries or fiduciaries, or decide to otherwise drastically amend your plan, then modifications are in order (see Chapter 3 for more on this).

QUESTION: *I assisted my elderly mother after my father died, so I understand the importance of having an "advocate" who can step in when needed to handle things for an elderly or disabled person. This includes such matters as health issues, "con man" attacks, financial scams, care services, contacts with agencies, etc. My wife and I are concerned that, in the future, if one or both of us is unable to handle our own affairs, we'll have no one to help because no responsible family member will be available to step in. Can we prearrange our own care with an agency that can be depended upon to supply these kinds of advocacy services at a reasonable cost? If so, how do we find and screen them?*

ANSWER: If all that you needed was help to manage your financial affairs, we'd suggest contacting the trust department of a small bank where you live, which could arrange to provide the fiduciary services that you and your wife might need in the future. But finding an experienced advocate who could provide the number of wide-ranging services you describe is a different kettle of fish.

A large national bank that we contacted said they don't provide advocacy services per se. Geriatric care managers are professionals, such as social workers, counselors, nurses, or gerontologists, who specialize in assisting older people and their families to attain the highest quality of life, given their circumstances.

According to the National Association of Professional Geriatric Care Managers (GCM), geriatric care managers can conduct care planning assessments; screen, arrange, and monitor in-home help or other services; review financial, legal, or medical issues and offer referrals to geriatric specialists; provide crisis intervention; monitor a loved one's care in a hospital or nursing home; act as a liaison to families at a distance; assist with moving an older person to or from a retirement complex, assisted-care home, or nursing home; provide consumer education and advocacy; and offer counseling and support. Some geriatric care managers also provide family or individual therapy, finance management, and conservatorship or guardianship assistance and/or caregiving services. Some of these firms also provide these services for the disabled.

GCM, based in Tucson, Arizona, can provide you with a list of its more than 1,500 members. But the catch is that unlike, say, the American Medical Association, GCM itself has no specific certification or licensing requirements. In fact, non-voting members, called "affiliates," need only have a high-school diploma. So there's no guarantee that the person/firm you hire is actually qualified to do what you need it to do.

There's also the question of cost. Good geriatric care managers don't come cheap; many charge at least $90 an hour. But a good one may be worth every penny.

GCM suggests asking several questions when screening a potential geriatric care manager, including: What are your professional credentials? Are you licensed in your profession? How long have you been in business? Are you available for emergencies? Does your company also provide home-care services? How do you communicate information to me? What are your fees? (These should be provided in writing to the consumer/responsible party prior to initiating services.) Can you provide me with references?

Senior Matters Consulting, Inc. (**www.seniormatters. net**) offers an additional tip. Ask for a referral list of professionals (physicians, attorneys, social service workers) in your area who have actually worked with the geriatric care manager in question and who can substantiate the quality of the work that the manager performs.

You could also contact GCM (**www.caremanager.org**), or perhaps the employee assistance program where you are employed, and put them to work for you. Ask them to recommend a firm that you could hire for future reference, and specify that you would need someone with a master's degree or a certified-nurse level of care. Then, keep those references handy for the future, when you or your wife might need them.

SECTION II:
Preparing the Necessary Documents

3

What You'll Need for Your Plan

No matter who you are, you need three basic documents:

- a durable financial power of attorney,
- a durable health care power of attorney, and
- a will that includes trust provisions, especially if there are minors or disabled individuals involved.

While we are going to repeat, in part, some definitions of these documents later, the descriptions in other portions of this book are used in a special context—for example, in the situation of unmarried cohabitants.

Durable Financial Power of Attorney

A power of attorney is a written document by which you give a trusted person over age 18—called an attorney-in-fact, a proxy, or an agent—the legal authority to act for you under certain circumstances. All fifty states authorize these documents through which you control the authority granted to your agent and under what conditions the power may be exercised.

A power of attorney is "durable" so long as it contains the "magic language" that allows your agent to handle your affairs if you become incapacitated. If this language is not included, your agent will have no authority to handle your affairs if you become incapacitated, necessitating a conservatorship or guardianship proceeding in the probate court. An example of the "magic language" is:

> This Power of Attorney shall not be affected by my physical disability or mental incompetence which renders me incapable of managing my own estate.

By including this language, your agent's authority begins when you sign, remains in effect even if you become incapacitated, and terminates on your death, at which time your will takes over. If you don't want your agent's authority to become effective until you become incapacitated, then you may want to consider a "springing durable power of attorney," which provides that the agent's authority "springs" into effect when you become unable to act for yourself as determined by your doctor.

We highly recommend that powers of attorney be drafted to suit your individual needs. While such a document is more expensive, when you get to the point that it must be used, you want a Hummer, not a Ford Fiesta. You should also discuss with your attorney gifting provisions—that is, whether your agent should be allowed to make gifts to third persons, including himself or herself, upon your incapacity. While gifting to spouses in unlimited amounts is a good thing for Medicaid planning, particularly where you have a long-term marriage, if you have a short-term marriage it might be disastrous. Note that you can change or cancel a power of attorney at any time after you sign it, so long as you still have mental capacity and follow the law of your state of residence.

Durable Health-Care Power of Attorney

"Advance Health-Care Directives" refer to a number of documents you can use to express your wishes about your future medical treatment should you become incapacitated. These documents do not take effect until you become incapacitated and are unable to make decisions. Until then, you can change or revoke the document. In effect, durable health-care powers of attorney are actually springing durable powers of attorney that allow the agent to act when you (the "principal") are incapacitated.

Through a durable health-care power of attorney, you can direct that *everything* possible be done to preserve your life, that *nothing* be done, or that some procedures be done and others not be done. You can make the document flexible enough to deal with unforeseen developments by giving your agent the authority to act as he or she sees fit, or you can specifically limit your agent's authority to act.

Your Will

Through your will, you control what happens to your property at the time of your death. Since a will does not become effective until you die, you may change or cancel it at any time after you sign it, so long as you still have mental capacity and follow the law of the state where you live. Without a will, you forfeit your right to direct where your property goes when you die. This is especially important if you are living with a partner to whom you are not married, since the surviving partner will then receive nothing. Without a will, unintended results will occur.

In addition to directing how your probate property is distributed after your death, your will also names the individual whom you trust to administer your estate. Your will can also include burial instructions, appoint trustees, and, depending on how your will is prepared, even be able to save your estate from taxes. You can also include a so-called "in terrorem" clause, meaning that if any beneficiary challenges your will, he or she will be subject to economic penalties.

Living Trust

A living trust is a revocable trust that you can change or terminate at any time while you are competent. If properly prepared and implemented, a living trust can allow you to carry out your wishes in both life and death, leave you in charge of your wealth until you die, and avoid probate. Before you choose to use a revocable living trust, however, you should make sure you understand the long-term effects and what it will and won't do for you and your partner, if you have one.

Since there will be no tax benefits involved if you choose to use a living trust, your estate will still include whatever assets may be transferred into the trust. If you choose to use a living trust, we suggest that you use a qualified lawyer and beware of trust mills that overcharge for these documents. If you use a will, you will hold title to your assets during your lifetime, and your will provides who gets what and when. If you use a living trust, your assets belong to the trustees for your benefit, and are distributed as stated in your living trust. Even if you have a living trust, you will need a will that "pours over" assets you may have forgotten to transfer to the living trust.

Whom to Choose as Your Fiduciary

When you choose an agent to serve under your financial or health power of attorney or a personal representative to handle your estate, you want to try to be certain that if and when your fiduciary is later called on to implement your decisions, he or she will be able to act effectively on your behalf and, it is hoped, eliminate family disputes. Therefore, whom you appoint is one of your most important decisions before signing any document. No matter whom you choose, you should fully discuss your wishes with your fiduciary and provide him or her with your documents.

If necessary, you can make your documents sufficiently flexible to either expand or limit your fiduciary's authority to act. When making decisions about what person to choose, think about the following:

- If you're considering naming your first spouse, is he/she capable? Will he/she be pressured by the children or others?

- If you're considering naming your second or subsequent spouse, is this a short-term or long-term spouse? Are there children from this marriage, as well, who may not be provided for?

- If you're considering naming grown children, do they any have debt, alcohol, drug, or marital problems? If so, they are "No-No's." If there is a trust for a disabled sibling, it is generally not a good idea to make another sibling the trustee because of potential conflicts, especially if the proposed trustee is also a beneficiary. Distance from your residence is also a relevant consideration.

You could also name:

- other relatives,

- friends,

- corporate fiduciaries: There are many small trust companies that will handle smaller estates and act as agents instead of a family member. In our view, small corporate fiduciaries tend to help prevent family disputes.

Where to Put Your Documents

After you sign your documents, you should put your will in your safe-deposit box or in a fireproof place at home. Make sure your personal representative knows where the will is located and has the ability to secure the original document when you die. Generally, the original will is required to probate an estate although, under limited circumstances, copies can be used. Without the original, however, needless attorney's fees will be incurred.

Your durable power of attorney should be recorded among the public records in your county of residence, and copies should be provided to your agent(s). Copies of your health-care documents should be given to your doctor and agent(s) because this document will do you no good if those whom you want to make decisions don't have the papers.

Will Substitutes

Rather than preparing wills, some individuals prefer not to pay lawyers and to use, instead, what are generally called "will substitutes," such as joint accounts, beneficiary designations on insurance, annuities, IRAs, and other retirement funds. But by placing a person's name on your bank or brokerage account, you give that individual complete control over that account. This means that person could take the entire account and leave the country. It also means that if you become incapacitated and die, that account becomes the property of the joint account holder.

We believe that the better course is to place an individual's name on your accounts as your "agent" or "attorney in fact," so that that person has a fiduciary responsibility to you. And at your death, the account passes under your will, not to that person.

What Else to Do?

Now that you have worked through the options and completed your life and estate planning process, you can stop thinking about it and relax in the knowledge that your estate planning is complete—right?

Almost! While you can enjoy the peace of mind that flows from completion of the project, the truth is that your life and estate planning needs may need to be revisited regularly. How often? Most lawyers will say that you should review, and possibly revise, your life and estate plans every five years. While five years may sound like a short time period, think a minute about what your life was like five or ten years ago, and how much has changed. Maybe your children have grown up, gone to college, or started their own families during that time. Maybe you have retired, changed careers, or moved to a new city or state. Maybe you are worth significantly more—or less—than you were then. Maybe you or your spouse have had some health problems that require modification of your plans.

In addition, none of us knows how much change there will be in the legal system during the same time frame. For example, the portion of your estate that may be subject to federal and state estate taxes has changed radically, but after 2010, no one knows what it will be until Congress passes, and the President signs, a new law. If your estate plan includes a pattern of making gifts to children and grandchildren, the amount of those gifts that can be made without gift tax implications each year has increased over the years from $10,000 per person to $13,000 per recipient (the latter is the amount for 2009). Due to uncertain economic times in America and, for that matter, the world, no one can guess what the annual exclusion may be down the road.

In light of the difficult stock market environment, it is very challenging to try to guess how much any of us will be worth five years from now. It is probably much more difficult to guess—and it would be a guess—how financially self-reliant children, spouses, and other family members will be, or how well they will be able to handle an inheritance.

So, when specifically should you revisit your estate and life-planning choices? The answer varies somewhat depending on your circumstances, but here are some specific life changes that ought to get you thinking about a visit with your attorney:

- Birth of a child or grandchild (especially the first occurrence of either).

- Death or disability of a spouse or child.

- Divorce or remarriage by you and possibly your child; however, there is no need to change your plan just because a child changes her or his name as a result of marriage or divorce.

- Receipt of a substantial inheritance, or any other significant change in financial status.

- Retirement.

- A move to a new state, or purchase of a second residence in another state, even though you do not change your primary residence.

- Learning that a child or grandchild has a disability (especially one that might involve eligibility for public benefits or medical care).

In addition, you should make an appointment to discuss the effect of any significant changes in state or federal laws involving estate-planning issues. How will you know those have occurred? In addition to news reports and public discussions, you might hear about changes from your lawyer, who should be interested in letting you know about what is happening in the estate-planning world.

Any or all of these changes mean that your plan may require adjustment in order to stay in tune with your life circumstances.

QUESTION: *My wife and I are in our late 60s and have about $500,000 in assets. We don't anticipate paying estate taxes. We have one married child who has two children, both in high school. Every asset we own, including our home, is titled jointly with right of survivorship so that if I die first, she gets it all, and if she dies first, I get it all. Our small life insurance policies and IRAs go to each other as beneficiary. Given our planning, is there any reason for us to go to the expense of getting wills drawn up?*

ANSWER: Assuming, as you say, that all assets are jointly titled with right of survivorship at the death of the first of you, each of the assets titled in this fashion will pass to the survivor automatically. This means, at the first death, there will be no probate assets to go through the estate process. If, on the other hand, there are assets not titled in this fashion—like an automobile—there will be some red tape involved in getting title to that asset passed. While under these very limited circumstances wills may not be necessary for the first of you to die, the survivor will probably need a will to make sure that assets go where they are intended to go. For example, if the second of you dies without a will and your son is disabled or has died before you, there may be an unintended result.

QUESTION: *My husband and I have been married for 51 years, and he refuses to see a lawyer to get his will drawn up even though he owns everything. He says that I shouldn't worry because I get what he calls a "wife's share." We have five children. I have never worked outside the home. He has* *a house, some furniture, savings, and a small retirement. What happens if he dies first and has no will?*

ANSWER: If your husband dies before you and has no will, the law of the state where you live dictates who inherits the house and the savings and in what proportions, regardless of your husband's intent. This means that if your husband owns all of the assets and dies before you, you will be in the unenviable position of owning all assets jointly with your five children or, in some instances, your grandchildren. This means really expensive problems to solve, much more expensive than the cost of a will.

Although you should check the law of the state in which you live, the following is an example of what happens in one state if a person dies without a will: (1) If married with no children, everything goes to the surviving spouse; (2) If married with children, one-half goes to the surviving spouse and one-half is divided equally among the children; (3) If unmarried with children, all goes to the children equally; (4) If not married and no children, all goes to surviving parents, and if parents are not surviving, to brothers and sisters equally with the child or children of a deceased sibling taking the share a parent would have taken; (4) If not married, no children, and no surviving parents or siblings, the law of the state defines what next of kin will inherit.

BOTTOM LINE: You and your husband need wills.

4

Potential Pitfalls and Lifelines

In the early stages of the planning process, it's important to be aware of numerous potential pitfalls that can throw a wrench into the machinery. A person's health, finances, or family situation can change in an instant, and this important fact of life needs to be understood from the very beginning of the planning process. In addition, the rules and regulations governing benefit programs are in a state of constant flux. When planning for the long term, therefore, flexibility is the key. The best plans generally don't depend on any one factor, such as the availability of Medicaid (the joint federal/state program for the poor and disabled). So plans must be as redundant as possible.

Health Insurance Blues

Health insurance, if you have not yet turned 65, is essential. Continuation through an employer's health plan may be pricey; on the other hand, an individual health insurance policy may be unavailable.

Durable Power of Attorney: Do It Right

Guardianships and/or conservatorships are comparatively poor, yet ultra-expensive substitutes for good health and financial planning. Remember, it may be difficult to convince a judge to allow transfers of assets from an incapacitated adult, and all other transactions and expenditures would be subject to court scrutiny. This may result in costly and time-consuming hearings while a long-term care plan is being developed and/or implemented.

An inappropriately drafted durable power of attorney can be deadly. This problem is avoidable if the senior signs a comprehensive durable power of attorney early enough in the process so that a trusted third person can make the transfers or expenditures when needed. So long as the senior has the capacity to name agents, the execution of a properly drafted power of attorney should be the first priority in any type of planning.

In addition, since standard powers granting discretion to the agent are not sufficient to allow the agent to make gifts to himself or herself or to others, specific authority must be granted in the power of attorney sufficient to accomplish the planning goals. Generally, this means that appropriate "gifting powers" must be expressly stated within the document. Great care must be used in granting gifting authority, and this should only be done with the help of an experienced attorney who understands your needs.

The power of attorney should not be downloaded from the Internet, and it should not be a "one-size-fits-all" document. Once the situation has been evaluated by an experienced attorney, appropriate gifting authority may be included in the power of attorney. However, be forewarned that an agent's power to make gifts to him or herself may be construed by the IRS as a general power of appointment, which carries with it certain tax implications.

Therefore, this language should not be included in instruments without assuring that the combined taxable estates of the principal and the agent are below taxable limits.

Long-Term Care Planning Is Rife with Conflicts

This is because the issue here is how to preserve assets for the ultimate beneficiaries (children, grandchildren, and so on), as opposed to the senior maintaining control over the assets for as long as possible. Addressing these conflicts is essential, particularly if the long-term care plan is Medicaid-based, because most planning techniques involve the elderly person giving up control of assets that he/she earned and turning them over to a child or children to hold. But there are downsides here. The child may abscond with or spend the money, be the subject of a judgment that could take the money, die and leave it to a spouse or child who won't do the right thing, or become divorced and lose or lessen the funds.

Therefore, the senior must assess his/her comfort level in giving up control of any assets. If he or she is uncomfortable with this aspect of the plan, and if this concern is not alleviated, there will have to be an alternate plan or the entire planning process will have to be abandoned. (Note, however, there are ways to place assets in a child's name with protections; this can be accomplished by an experienced attorney in this field.)

A second area of potential conflict is that of intra-family relations. As early as possible, it must be determined what the driving force is behind the decision to seek a long-term care plan. Was the decision made by the elder, a spouse, a second spouse, a child, or perhaps a caregiver to a person who has no close family? Perhaps it was the decision of all the children, or maybe just one. It must be determined whether the concerns of the senior and other involved family members are the same.

While the senior's goals must be the ultimate focus, this aspect of the planning process is not always clear. In order to accurately assess the senior's goals, the attorney must speak independently with the senior outside of the presence of the family. And, if there are potential physical or mental capacity issues, the senior should be medically assessed prior to signing documents.

A third area of potential conflict is the quality and type of care, as opposed to the cost of care. As with any other commodity, the more you get, the more it costs. The senior and the family must face the issue of how much care can be afforded and still meet the family's other financial needs. Should the senior stay at home? Does he/she need residential care or is home care a realistic option? Can the family afford to have sitters or can a nurse come into the house? Can a spouse or child take care of the senior? Does he/she need a residential care facility or nursing home care? And if so, how should the senior be approached and by whom? Should the senior have a private room?

Ultimately, the planning process comes down to the question of the senior's needs, as opposed to his or her desires. While almost no one wants to be in a nursing home, some people *need* to be in a nursing home in order to receive necessary care. The senior's perception of his/her health and abilities—as well as the ability of the family to provide appropriate care—may be very different from the realities of the situation.

You Can't Always Depend on Receiving Medicaid

Some middle-class elders think they can give away their assets or sell their house for "$5" and be safe. Or, give away $10,000 a year and be safe. This is not the case. Medicaid is a means-tested government benefit program, meaning that an individual's or couple's assets and income are relevant in determining whether that person receives the benefit. If an asset is determined to be "available," it is countable against the applicant unless that asset is specifically exempt or disregarded. If an asset can be sold for money without the consent of another and is not exempt, it is considered to be available.

If elders transfer or give away assets for less than fair market value, this can result in a period of ineligibility for Medicaid coverage for long-term care services, although this may not be the case for other Medicaid programs. On the other hand, given sufficient "lead time" in the planning process, experienced planners may determine that even if penalties are imposed, they will be of little or no practical significance. The planner must also be on the lookout for transactions that may unexpectedly produce penalties. For example, if a daughter has cared for a parent for five years and the parent decides to pay her for her trouble by transferring $50,000 to her just before entering a nursing home, this payment would produce a sanction period if the parent applied for Medicaid immediately thereafter. Still, with sufficient lead time and appropriate planning and documents, these types of unpleasant surprises can be avoided.

Medicaid Is Not Always the Best Option

Tax consequences generated in long-term care planning may result in winning the Medicaid eligibility battle but losing the overall war of the true economic impact. For individuals or couples with significant assets who can afford to pay privately, private pay may be the best option, especially if income levels are high enough that a rapid depletion of assets in not likely and/or the Medicaid savings would be minimal.

Remember, the federal government wants repayment of Medicaid expenditures after the death of the recipient. Because the federal government has placed mandates on states to recover after death the Medicaid benefits that were paid to recipients during their lives, the potential of an estate recovery claim by Medicaid produces increasing pressure from children and family members for the senior or senior couple to make early and outright transfers of such properties, which is not always the best thing to do.

Planning Tools Can Trigger Taxation Effects

If, for example, you sign a contract to pay your daughter for providing care for you, the payments to your daughter will be taxable income to her, not a gift. In addition, she may be your employee, thus requiring you to pay state and federal taxation, including unemployment, Social Security, and so on. On the other hand, should you make an outright gift of more than your annual exclusion (at present, $13,000 per person to any number of individuals in any one year), you will be required to file gift tax returns. And gifts can be tricky.

The gift of an asset other than cash passes at your (the donor's) cost basis, thus exposing the recipient (donee) with exposure to capital gains taxes upon sale. For example, if you give your son 100 shares of stock valued at $120 per share for which you paid $20 per share, while the gift amount is $2,000.00, if your son sells the 100 shares for $120 per share ($12,000.00), he will incur and be required to pay capital gains taxes on the difference between the $120 sales price and your $20 cost basis in the stock—or $100 per share. Therefore, on sale your son would be required to pay state and federal income taxes at the capital gains rate on a $12,000.00 gift that is valued by the government for tax purposes as being worth $2,000.00. On the other hand, if your son inherited this stock from you after your death and sold it for $120 per share, under current law, there would be no capital gains taxes due.

IRAs and 401(k)s Carry with Them Their Own Problems

Because income tax has been deferred on contributions to and growth of assets in these types of accounts, the funds you contribute grow without being taxed. Therefore, when you begin making withdrawals, you will be assessed with income taxes. In addition to taxation issues when withdrawn, these types of accounts pose severe problems in Medicaid planning, particularly when owned by the institutionalized spouse who, under federal law, can't have more than $2,000 in countable resources in his/her own name. Therefore, the holder of these types of assets who is institutionalized will be required to withdraw the entire account balance, pay income taxes, and potentially pay penalties for early withdrawal of these funds. Because each situation is different, advice from an experienced attorney and certified public accountant is essential.

Not Having the Proper Documents in Place Is a Disaster Waiting to Happen

A common problem in all types of planning is that desirable transfers can't be made when they need to be made. Why not? Because the person who owns the asset lacks the legal capacity to make the transfer and has not properly authorized a trusted third person to act for him or her. In other words, if Mom and Dad, like many seniors, refuse to entrust decision-making authority to their children, a trusted relative, or a bank trust department by using a revocable trust or durable power of attorney, should either or both become incapacitated to the extent that they can't handle their business, the family will be forced to resort to the probate or surrogate court to have a fiduciary appointed. This is an unnecessary and expensive alternative to an appropriate trust or power of attorney.

Estate Planning Is in Flux

Although Congress voted to repeal the federal estate and genera-
tion-skipping tax in 2001 through a gradual phase-out, this legislation won't affect most families who are having difficulty paying
for their long-term care. That's because only about 1 percent of
Americans who die each year have large enough estates to file an
estate tax return. Moreover, unless Congress acts, in 2011 the estate
tax will be reinstated, with an exclusion of $1 million. Ordinary
folks, however, won't be gifting their progeny large amounts of
money; most middle-class couples need to retain control over every
penny to ensure they have sufficient funds in the event one or both
needs long-term care. Caveat: At the writing of this publication, our
economy is in a mess, and no one knows what Congress and the
President will do with estate, capital gains, and income taxes, given
the huge national debt.

Wills Are Not Foolproof

Because non-probate assets are transferred at death based upon
title or beneficiary designation, the will does not always do what
the deceased person intended. In other words, since life insurance,
IRAs, annuities, joint-with-right-of-survivorship accounts, beneficiaries of revocable trusts, contractual devices, and retirement plan
proceeds are paid directly to beneficiaries outside of the decedent's
will, structuring the beneficiary designations for non-probate assets
is most important.

For example, it is not unusual for a person to place the name of
a child or another trusted loved one on an account for administrative purposes, not understanding that at death this account will
belong totally to the person whose name was placed upon the title.
The planning process, therefore, should include learning about and

discussing the appropriate use of techniques that allow assets to pass to a beneficiary outside of a will and without the necessity of probate. Moreover, while real estate and other assets held jointly with right of survivorship will pass outright to the survivor without going through probate, the family must be advised about risks inherent in a joint-tenancy, including (aside from adverse income tax consequences) separation, divorce, death, or incapacity that are not anticipated.

For example, in most states, a letter to the bank and/or a statement in your will that you have no intent to give ownership to an individual whose name is listed on your account should solve the problem. However, it is best not to place others' names on accounts unless you really understand what you are doing. By using an appropriate power of attorney, you can avoid this unintended result.

Retirement Plans Are Complex

To engage in appropriate planning, first the senior and spouse must determine the age at which the wage earner(s) will retire, assuming neither has been involuntarily terminated. Using this calculation, the planner must then consider Social Security, pensions, IRAs, investment earnings, spouse's earnings, and the like—in addition to whether the pension should be taken in a lump sum rollover or annuitized. Additionally, depending on the health of the non-working spouse, should he or she be made the survivor beneficiary?

Lump sum distributions from qualified retirement plans can be complicated. If the retiree rolls over all or part of the distribution to an IRA, no tax will be due on the part rolled over. If the retiree takes any part of the plan, however, he or she must report the entire taxable part of the distribution as ordinary income. For some, there may be a special 10-year averaging rule to determine the tax on the taxable part of the distribution.

If the retiree is under age 59½, the 10 percent penalty that would normally be imposed can be avoided if the individual takes advantage of Section 72t of the Internal Revenue Code that authorizes what is known as substantially equal payments. In this way, the owner of the IRA or 401(k) can take a stream of substantially equal payments for five years or until reaching age 59½, whichever comes later, with no penalty, but income taxes will be due and payable.

A retiree can roll over all or part of a lump sum distribution into another qualified pension plan within sixty days after the distribution and continue to defer income tax on the portion rolled over. But unless the transfer is made directly from one trustee to another, 20 percent of the distribution will be withheld for income taxes, thereby reducing the amount available for rollover. In order to qualify the total distribution for tax-free rollover status, the retiree must then contribute from his or her own funds an amount equal to the tax withheld.

If the individual fails to arrange for a trustee-to-trustee distribution and withholding occurs, the person can recapture the amount withheld upon payment of his income taxes after the year is concluded. If, however, he has failed to contribute the amount withheld during the sixty-day period after the distribution, he will find that it is now too late to use the tax refund to make up the difference; the amount withheld is now taxable income for the year when it was received.

You Might End up Living with an Adult Child—or Vice Versa

Living with adult children is something many seniors, and their middle-age children, never thought about in their earlier years. Yet it's happening more frequently because of difficult economic times, mounting debts, loss of employment, the death of a spouse, health concerns, or one parent entering an assisted-living facility or a nursing home. And, it happens both ways: Sometimes seniors show up on their children's doorsteps; sometimes it's the other way around.

No matter who moves where, it is absolutely essential that there be financial, social, and other parameters drawn in order to govern these unusual living arrangements. And even though you are family, the conditions dealing with the living arrangements should be put in writing.

First, who is going to pay what household bills? If monthly obligations—such as the mortgage payment, garbage, taxes, and insurance—are not affected by the number of people in the home, then these should not be divided. In order to avoid payments being classified as taxable rent to the recipient, an expense-sharing agreement to set the parameters should be prepared by a knowledgeable lawyer.

Second, if the residence needs added space, construction costs can be handled in a number of ways, including loans, purchase of a life interest, and other types of arrangements. To be valid, actuarial tables must be used to determine life interests. As the purchaser of a life interest gets older, the value of the life interest reduces in value. Generally, the owner of the life interest pays the taxes, insurance, and upkeep on the residence. If family members pay for repairs voluntarily, there may be gift tax implications, depending on how the transaction is done. An experienced lawyer is required to deal with these intricate planning opportunities.

Third, getting along is essential. For that reason, each keeping up his/her part of the bargain regarding cleaning, not smoking, and having overnight guests is important in order to keep the relationship on an even keel.

Fourth, the senior and the grown child should each take care of their own finances. If one child moves in with Mom, the other children may become convinced—rightly or wrongly—that the resident child is taking advantage of Mom. Therefore, it is best to keep the resident child out of Mom's finances.

Fifth, if a nursing home is required for the senior, the manner in which the living-together transaction was set up may mean the difference between the senior qualifying for Medicaid and not. That is why planning must be accomplished properly and put into writing. While sharing a home with a parent or middle-age child may not have been part of your plan, you must be flexible enough to fit this fast-developing phenomenon into your planning process.

Despite the many potential pitfalls seniors face, there are some *lifelines*, too. A reverse mortgage is one that is becoming increasingly popular.

Reverse Mortgages: A Good Resource If Used Properly

In the days before credit cards and easy credit, when we bought something we paid cash or waited until we had the cash to make the purchase. In those days, our personal residence was our most valuable asset, and our home equity was sacrosanct. Then came 401(k)s, IRAs, pensions, and other accounts that were, to a large degree, dependent on the up-and-down trends of the stock market. This led many Americans to financial advisors in an effort to secure higher and higher returns and, whether they realized it or not, greater and greater risks. Almost simultaneously, easy credit crept into our lives.

After years during which many Americans were not concerned about spending or the values of their assets, recent downward trends have decimated savings and retirements, reduced home values, and left many with high-interest credit card and other un-secured debt that can't be serviced with current income. If you find yourself in this position, or if you just need the availability of extra cash, you may be interested to know that more and more American homeowners over age 62 are considering reverse mortgages as a way to get rid of debt, create a pool of available cash, and have no obligation to repay the loan until death or the sale of the personal residence. While the decision of whether or not to use a reverse mortgage requires much more research and review than contained here, a concise explanation of the product and process may lead many of you in the right direction.

To qualify for a reverse mortgage, homeowners must be age 62 or older; must own and occupy the property as a primary residence which meets FHA standards; must engage in an informational counseling session; must maintain the property home with needed upkeep and make repairs required after the appraisal and inspec-tion; and must pay property taxes and insurance. There are no minimum income or credit requirements for reverse mortgages, and when the reverse mortgage is established, there are no restric-tions on how the funds are used. The amount of the loan is based on age of youngest owner/borrower, the existing interest rate, and the appraised value or the existing FHA insurance limit, whichever is less.

By using a reverse mortgage, homeowners who are 62 or older can use their home equity to obtain payouts in lump sum, a credit line, a series of set monthly payments, or a combination of the above. The borrower retains title to the property and continues to be responsible for property taxes, insurance premiums, and repairs and maintenance. While the payouts are free of income tax, receipt of the payout may make individuals ineligible for state and federal benefits, including Medicaid, unless the statutory law in the owner's state of residence creates an exception.

There are no payments due on the loan until the last owner/borrower moves out of the home, dies, or the home is sold. At the time of the event that triggers the payback, the mortgage debt, interest, and fees accruing over the life of the loan could exceed the remaining equity; however, under the terms of the mortgage, the loan repayment will never exceed the market value of the home, even if home prices continue to decline. This means that the ultimate beneficiaries of the estate won't be held responsible for any deficiency.

For example, if the residence is valued at $100,000 at the time of the $75,000 reverse mortgage, but is worth only $60,000 when the loan is paid, neither the owners nor their estates or heirs are liable for the deficiency.

However, those who qualify for reverse mortgages may be pressured into using the funds to purchase ill-advised annuities and other financial products that pay handsome commissions to unscrupulous advisors and also limit access to the funds. While newly enacted rules forbid lenders from requiring borrowers to buy financial products as a condition of the loan agreement, the risk of inappropriate use of funds is still there.

The major difference between a reverse mortgage and a second mortgage or home equity line of credit is that to qualify for a traditional line of credit, you must have sufficient income as opposed to debt ratio to qualify, and you must make monthly mortgage payments. On the other hand, the reverse mortgage pays the borrower despite your income and credit standing. The loan amount you can qualify for depends on your age, the current interest rate, and the lesser of appraised value of your home or FHA mortgage limits in your area. In other words, the more valuable your home, the older you are, and the lower the interest rate, the more you can borrow.

With a reverse mortgage, you won't make any payments, you can't be foreclosed upon, there is no repayment so long as the property remains your principal residence and one of the borrowers continues to stay in the home and pays taxes and insurance, and you will never owe more than the value of your residence. On the other hand, if your property increases in value after you take out a reverse mortgage, you may be able to secure a second or even third reverse mortgage using the increased home equity. The reverse mortgage(s) must be the only mortgage on your property.

At the time of your death or when you sell your primary residence, you or your estate is obligated to repay what you received, plus interest and fees. Any remaining equity belongs to you or to your heirs.

You should never pay any "estate planning service" or anyone else a fee for a referral to a lender because HUD (the federal Office of Housing and Urban Development) provides this information without cost. Effective November 1, 2008, the Homeownership Act of 2008 increased the limit on reverse mortgages and made those who have existing reverse mortgages eligible to take advantage of the higher lending limits. In addition, origination fees that were previously set at 2 percent of the loan amount are now capped at $6,000. And, for the first time, in 2009, qualifying individuals will be able to use a reverse mortgage to purchase a new home.

If you have a mortgage on your property, it will have to be paid off. If not, the entire loan proceeds will be available to you. We have seen most people decide to take the proceeds in a credit line and, when necessary to supplement monthly cash flow, to take down the amount necessary. For example, some choose to use the proceeds from the reverse mortgage to pay once-per-year or once-per-quarter obligations such as property taxes and property insurance. Others choose to pay their health insurance premiums, payments for prescription drugs, and even long-term care insurance premiums. While judicious use of these funds is suggested, some have unwisely used the funds to take vacations or provide for entertainment and quality-of-life expenses not otherwise available. If the proceeds are used in part to pay off high-interest credit cards, it is important not to make the same mistake twice; tear up those credit cards.

There are also public sector reverse mortgages—not funded by HUD—where the amount available generally depends on your age, your home's value and location, and the cost of the loan. The largest loans are generally made to the oldest borrowers who live in the most expensive homes, but these are dependent upon the plan or program selected, because loan amounts vary significantly from one plan to another. Generally, the largest cash advances are derived from the federally insured Home Equity Conversion Mortgage (HECM).

Home Equity Conversion Mortgages account for 90 percent of all reverse mortgages originated in the United States. While the upfront fees (which are taken from the reverse mortgage proceeds) are high, these costs are ameliorated by lower interest rates over the term of the loan. If you don't intend to remain in the home for more than five years, getting a reverse mortgage may not be a good idea. The expenses attributable to reverse mortgages are greater in the early years of the loan, but they become less costly over time. Therefore, the use of reverse mortgages should be based upon an intention to do so for the long haul, not for the short-term.

The unused funds that remain on your credit line can be moved into investments, if you desire; however, you can keep them with the lender, which generally pays more than the interest rate charged on the loan, or you can place your funds with a financial advisor which, in our view, is very risky in this economic climate where preservation of principal is essential. The interest rate on reverse mortgages is determined on a program-to-program basis because the loans are secured by your residence alone. Before 2007, the reverse mortgage programs used adjustable interest rates and a maximum cap. Now, some reverse mortgage lenders offer FHA HECM reverse mortgages with fixed rates.

When you apply for an FHA/HUD reverse mortgage, you will be required to engage in a 45-minute counseling session with a HUD-approved counselor, who will explain the legal and financial obligations involved. Once completed, you will receive a "certificate of counseling" that is required before the loan application can be processed.

According to the Internal Revenue Service, loan advances from reverse mortgages are not considered to be income, and interest charges are not deductible until the loan is actually paid off at the end of the loan. Depending on the program, the loan becomes due when the last homeowner dies, sells the house, or, depending on the loan conditions, leaves the house for twelve consecutive months (for example, the owner goes into an assisted-living facility or, due to physical or mental illness, is unable to stay at home).

In these events, if the borrower moves out or dies, so long as the borrower—or the estate—provides proof to the lender that he/she is attempting to sell the home or obtain financing to pay off the outstanding debt, the lender will allow up to a year to do so.

For further information, you can go to **www.hud.gov/ buying/rvrsmort.cfm**.

QUESTION: *I am 54. My husband, age 67, suffered a stroke three months ago that resulted in permanent brain damage and paralysis on the left side. He is being tube-fed, can't swallow on his own, and can't communicate at all. I need to transfer some of our assets to myself so that I can afford to live and also take care of my husband, but he never signed a power of attorney before he got sick. The upshot is that a judge appointed me as guardian. He also appointed a lawyer for my husband. The lawyer told the judge that since I was a fiduciary for my husband, I should not be allowed to make any transfers of our assets to myself, but that if I had to sell our house, I could have part of the equity. My lawyer says there is nothing else I can do to protect my husband and myself. Is this true?*

ANSWER: Ask the judge to reconsider, or appeal the decision. Both federal and state Medicaid laws, as well as public policy, allow intra-spousal transfers. And as your husband's guardian, not to allow you to make the transfers that your husband could have made if he had the capacity discriminates against him as an incapacitated person under the equal protection clause of the Constitution.

Federal Medicaid law sets minimum and maximum amounts of countable assets that can be set aside to the spouse in the community to take care of himself or herself and still allow the nursing home spouse to qualify for Medicaid assistance, called the "Community Spouse Resource Allowance." Each state establishes its own limit within the federal guidelines. This amount does not include the value of the family home and some other noncountable resources. Since you have an actuarial life expectancy of more than 25 years, no one could validly argue that the transfer of the home, plus your state's spousal resource allowance, will provide you with a life of leisure during your declining years.

While federal Medicaid law requires that states declare a Medicaid applicant ineligible if he or she disposes of assets for less than fair market value within a 36-month "look-back period" before the date of the application, the law also provides that it is contrary to public policy to force a community spouse such as you to use all marital assets to support your institutionalized spouse with resultant impoverishment of and public support for both of you instead of just one. Therefore, there is no Medicaid ineligibility if an institutionalized person transfers his or her principal place of residence to a spouse.

TAKING THE NEXTSTEP: This reader's dilemma could have been solved had her husband signed a durable power of attorney with spousal gifting provisions. Had he done so, the court proceeding would not have been necessary and significant dollars and time could have been saved.

5

Asset Management Tools

Now you are aware of the numerous snares that can await you during the planning process. While a competent professional team should be able to help you avoid those pitfalls, unless you remain in control and make sure your needs are addressed, your documents may well be next to useless.

There is always the possibility that at some point in your life you will become incapable of managing your own financial affairs. If this occurs and you don't have the necessary documents in place, judicial arrangements will have to be made for handling your income and assets. In order to avoid the expense and difficulty of judicial proceedings, there are several tools available for your use, each with its own particular benefits and drawbacks.

Tools for Use During Life

Joint Ownership of Assets—A Dangerous Management Tool

Many people choose to own property jointly with another person or persons. But by placing another person's name on an account, be aware that now that person has the authority to access the funds in that account.

Joint ownership arrangements can include a "right of survivorship," meaning that when one owner dies, the jointly owned property passes directly to the other listed owner(s). Under the right set of limited circumstances, joint ownership can be a simple method of addressing an asset management problem. For example, if you have no spouse and only one child or grandchild whom you trust, placing that person's name on your account as a joint owner can provide a number of advantages: You avoid probate, assets are passed quickly to the survivor (who is named co-owner), and a degree of availability is retained in the event of incapacity of one of the co-owners.

Joint ownership, however, also has the potential to lead to abuse and significant, unwanted problems. Consider the following example: Mary and Tom, sister and brother, own a checking account and certificates of deposit (CDs) jointly. These are funds that were inherited from their parents, and the funds have been titled this way for years. Mary has no children. Tom has one son, Tom, Jr., who is the sole beneficiary under the elder Tom's will. When Tom died, the accounts he owned jointly with Mary passed directly to her outside of probate and outside of the provisions of Tom's will. Tom, Jr. received no benefit from these accounts. When Mary dies, provided she owns the checking account and CDs in her name alone, they will pass through probate and be distributed according to her will. Thus, Tom, Jr. may never receive a share of these assets even though that is not what his father may have wanted.

Assuming that a portion of these assets remain at Mary's death, she could leave them to Tom, Jr. in her will, which would have to go through the probate process. To avoid probate at her death, Mary could make her nephew, Tom, Jr., a joint owner of the accounts. But in doing so, she runs the risk that Tom, Jr. may withdraw all of the money from these accounts while Mary is still living and dependent on these funds. If Tom, Jr. can be trusted, this is not a problem. If he cannot be trusted, however, or if he has financial problems, Mary could lose everything because these accounts could be exposed to the claims of young Tom's creditors if he fails to pay his debts or if he faces a money judgment after losing a lawsuit.

As these examples indicate, joint ownership of assets can pose many risks. It is imperative to think carefully, and to weigh the pros and cons, before using this particular tool.

Trusts

In general, a trust is an agreement between a "grantor" (sometimes called a "settlor") and an individual who will act as "trustee." The trust agreement also names one or more "beneficiaries" of the trust. So, Jim could create a trust as grantor for his benefit and the benefit of his wife, Joan. Jim could name himself and/or Joan or another person or entity as trustee. As grantor, Jim would transfer assets to the trustee, who is obligated to manage those assets for the designated trust beneficiaries according to the terms of the trust agreement. A trust agreement is almost always in writing, and it usually contains detailed instructions with respect to what the trustee can and can't do in managing the trust funds and in using them for the benefit of the beneficiary/beneficiaries.

In addition to one or more primary beneficiaries who would get lifetime benefits from the trust, a trust may also name secondary beneficiaries (also called "remainder beneficiaries" or "remaindermen") who may eventually benefit from the trust at some point in the future, e.g., at the death of the primary beneficiary. So, for example, Jim's trust could provide for both himself and his wife during their lives, for his wife during her life, and then for their children at her death.

Trusts may have multiple grantors (e.g., a mother and father who jointly establish a trust for their children's benefit), as well as multiple beneficiaries. A trust that a grantor establishes for his own benefit (meaning he names himself as the beneficiary) is known as a "grantor trust." This type of trust can be revocable or irrevocable.

Trusts can be very flexible mechanisms for dealing with asset management problems. They can also be a valuable tool in the estate planning process, since assets held in trust are generally not subject to probate. A trust created under the terms of a will is known as a "testamentary" trust. A trust created by an individual during his lifetime is known as an "*inter vivos*" trust, which is popularly known as a "living trust." It is generally revocable, and it is established for the benefit of the grantor and/or his family members.

One of the most useful reasons for establishing a living trust for elderly individuals is asset management. When a living trust is established, an individual can serve as trustee of his own trust, or a family member, friend, or corporate entity can be designated and immediately be given the responsibility of investing the assets and making all the management decisions for the person with respect to those investments.

For a person who is not capable of, or has no desire to be involved in the day-to-day decisions concerning investment of his assets, a living trust can be a useful vehicle to transfer those decisions and responsibilities to another while retaining the right to revoke the arrangement or replace the trustee at any time. By doing so, any assets in the living trust can continue to be invested and disposed of according to the terms of the trust in spite of the grantor's incapacity.

Although a power of attorney could give the same investment authority and also the authority to disburse assets as found in the living trust, the living trust may be more recognizable and more accepted by some third parties than a power of attorney.

In addition to asset management, the most often mentioned reasons for establishing a living trust are: (1) avoiding or reducing probate costs in states where the cost of probate is significant; (2) preserving privacy regarding the nature of assets; and (3) allowing a third party to manage the assets. Contrary to popular belief, living trusts have nothing to do with saving estate taxes.

Unfortunately, many individuals may have been "oversold" on these benefits. The advantages of a living trust should be weighed against the expense, time, and inconvenience involved in establishing the trust, re-titling property into the name of the trustee, and keeping accurate records of the trust property and its income. An additional income tax return may also be required on an annual basis.

Power of Attorney

A general durable power of attorney is a document whereby one person (the "principal") grants another person (the "agent" or "attorney-in-fact") the right to manage the principal's assets and to otherwise conduct his affairs. Under the law, the agent is said to "stand in the shoes of" the principal and has the right to deal with the principal's assets as if he/she were the principal, with a few exceptions. The primary exception is that the agent must act in the principal's best interest. This means that without a specific grant of authority, the agent can't use the power of attorney to make gifts—even if it does contain "catch-all" language about the agent being authorized to do anything that the principal could have done for himself.

A power of attorney may be designed to take effect immediately upon signing, or its effectiveness may be tied to some triggering event such as the incapacity of the principal. A power of attorney that only becomes effective upon the occurrence of such a triggering event is known as a "springing" durable power of attorney. It is very important that the power of attorney be "durable" (i.e., has language that causes the power to survive the principal's incompetency or incapacity). Additionally, once the principal becomes incompetent or incapacitated, the power of attorney must be recorded like a deed at the county courthouse in order to remain effective. A power of attorney expires upon the death of the principal. When the principal dies, the agent is no longer authorized to conduct the principal's business affairs, and the personal representative of the estate must be appointed/confirmed by the probate court to act for the estate.

A durable power of attorney is a flexible tool for addressing asset management issues. However, conferring such broad authority on another person also carries with it the potential for abuse, particularly if the agent is given extensive powers to make gifts. Great care, therefore, should be taken to choose an agent who is trustworthy and whose personal circumstances do not present a temptation to misuse the authority granted under the power of attorney. If desired as an added measure of protection, the power of attorney document may require the agent to give periodic accountings to an independent third party, such as a certified public accountant.

In lieu of a broad general power of attorney, a principal may choose to employ a limited power of attorney that only authorizes the agent to conduct specified transactions or types of activities. Although this type of arrangement may be useful in handling some situations, it obviously lacks the flexibility of a general power of attorney.

Without a durable power of attorney or a trust, a person's incapacity may lead to the following serious, difficult, and expensive consequences in the judicial arena:

A **conservatorship** is a protective arrangement established through a probate court proceeding. Once the probate judge is convinced that an individual is no longer capable of handling his own affairs based upon the sworn affidavits of medical examiners appointed by the court, the judge may appoint a conservator to manage the individual's finances in much the same way that an agent would do under a durable power of attorney. However, the court may choose to grant the conservator much less discretion and may impose strict reporting requirements, as well as require prior approval for many types of expenditures. Even in situations where a husband becomes incapacitated and never signed a durable power of attorney in favor of his wife, unless she is on the accounts, she has no authority to do anything and will be required to apply for conservatorship.

The considerable time and expense that may be involved in having a conservator appointed, the public nature of the proceeding, and the probable lack of flexibility make a conservatorship a less-than-favored option for asset management. In addition, since all interested persons must be notified, family members may come out of the woodwork to attempt to take over the finances of the family. This often pits brother against mother against sister.

A conservator is responsible for protecting ("conserving") the property of the incapacitated person. A guardian, on the other hand, is appointed by the probate court to take responsibility for the person.

A **guardianship** is similar to a conservatorship except that it focuses on the protection of the individual instead of his property. Once the probate judge is convinced that an individual is no longer capable of caring for himself, a protective arrangement is created through the appointment of a guardian. The guardian will generally have the same powers, rights, and duties with respect to the protected person that a parent has over a minor child, although the court does have the power to limit the guardian's authority to act.

The same individual may be appointed to serve as both guardian and conservator. Like conservatorships, guardianship proceedings may involve considerable time and expense, and they are also public in nature.

In some states, only one fiduciary is appointed by the court to handle both health-care and financial issues. No matter the situation, the fiduciary handling the finances will be required to account to the court.

Tools for After Your Death

Contrary to popular belief, you can, in fact, manage your assets from the grave. Your tools? A will and the probate process.

Wills

A will is a legal document that gives instructions about how your property should pass to your chosen beneficiaries after your death. For a will to be valid, it must comply with the signature and witnessing requirements of your state of residence. Generally, witnesses should not be related to you or be beneficiaries under your will. "Beneficiaries" are either people or organizations who will benefit from your assets after you die. Your will should describe your property and specify the amount or share that passes to each beneficiary. If you have minor children, your will is also the means by which to name your choice of a guardian for your children and a trustee for the funds that may pass to them under your will.

Your will should also name an individual or entity to act as the personal representative for your estate. The personal representative is responsible for paying your bills and carrying out the instructions in your will. While many nominate a close relative or friend as their personal representative, some choose a bank trust department, especially when funds are being left in trust for a disabled beneficiary, when funds are to be held in trust for minors because the parents are not trustworthy, or when there is a desire to avoid putting one family member at odds with another over how assets are distributed.

Since your will is not final until you die, until that time, your will has no legal significance. As such, you can alter, amend, or revoke it so long as you have mental capacity and follow the law of your state. An amendment to your will can be accomplished either by a "codicil" or by drawing up a new will. Generally, you can revoke your will either by (1) writing "revoked" on the face of the will, (2) drafting and signing a new will, (3) drafting and signing a written revocation, or (4) destroying your will with the intent to revoke it.

You have no obligation to leave assets to your children by will, but under the law of all states there are certain minimums you must leave to your spouse unless there has been a valid waiver accomplished under a premarital agreement or a separate document has been written after full financial disclosure has been made. This is especially important if your spouse is the result of a second, third, or further marriage. You should consider provisions in your will to deal with the potential that your spouse may be incapacitated when you die or may predecease you, in which event you should make sure to include alternate beneficiaries.

If you don't sign a will or trust, you will be deemed to have died "intestate," and your assets will pass according to the law of your state through the probate process.

Probate

Probate is the process by which the assets of a deceased person's estate—whether they leave a will or not—are inventoried and accounted for, debts and taxes are paid, and the remaining assets are passed to named beneficiaries and titled in their names.

It's important to understand that if you die without a will (or without a valid will), your state of residence, by law, determines who inherits your property. While the law of each state may have its own nuances, generally speaking:

- If you are married and have no children, all goes to your spouse.
- If you are married with children, one-half goes to the spouse and one-half to your children in equal shares.
- If you are not married and have children, all goes to the children equally.
- If you are not married and have no children, all goes to your parents if they are living. If no parent is living, your property goes to your brothers and sisters equally, with the children of a deceased sibling taking the share their parent would have taken.
- If you have no wife, children, parents, or siblings, the law of your state of residence defines your next of kin and in what order they stand to inherit.

Depending on where you live, the probate process can take a few months, or several years should complications arise. However, for most estates, the probate process lasts for one year or less. Contrary to popular belief, in most states, going through probate does not mean that your assets are tied up and your spouse will not be taken care of. In some states, however, such as California, New York, and New Jersey, probate costs are significant and attorneys charge steep percentages of estate value. In those states, a living trust may be a better solution.

The probate or surrogate court in your county of residence oversees the probate process, which consists of several steps. The first is "proving [that] the will" is valid and that no other will exists. In fact, the term "probate" comes from the Latin word meaning "to prove." A will must be presented to the probate court and its validity proven (i.e., it must be probated). If the will was not properly prepared or witnessed, the probate judge may decide to ignore the will's instructions and to proceed as if no will exists. If there is no will or the court refuses to recognize the will, then you will be determined to have died *intestate* ("without a will").

In addition to "proving the will," other steps in the probate process include: (1) officially confirming the personal representative named in the will, or appointing one if there is no will; (2) informing the interested parties—such as creditors, heirs, and beneficiaries—that the probate process has started; (3) filing an inventory and appraisal of the estate's assets; (4) paying creditors, taxes, and fees; (5) preparing a final accounting; (6) preparing a plan for distribution, and then distributing the remaining property to beneficiaries; and (7) closing the estate.

If a person dies with a will, the personal representative carries out the will's instructions by distributing the probate property as the deceased person specified in the will. If a person dies without a will, the court allots the property according to a formula set by state law. Thus, one good reason to write a will is to make sure that your probate property gets to people you wish, and not necessarily to the people set out in the state formula.

As previously noted, non-probate property passes to survivors outside the probate process and outside the terms of a will. In other words, the probate process won't be necessary if you die owning only the type of property called "non-probate property." This is property that is jointly owned and passes by law to the surviving co-owner(s) through what is known as right-of-survivorship. Non-probate property includes property that is held in trust, as well as jointly owned bank accounts, life insurance, annuities, pension benefits, IRAs, and other benefits that are paid to others who are named as beneficiaries. Non-probate assets may also include certain ownership interests in real estate.

On the other hand, property that is subject to the probate process is called "probate property." Generally, it includes (1) property that is owned and titled in your name alone; (2) property owned jointly without a right of survivorship (e.g., tenants in common); (3) life insurance paid to your estate, instead of to a specific person or organization; and (4) annuities and IRAs without named beneficiaries.

There might be other wrinkles, too, even if you have a valid will. For example, if a child is born to you after you make a will, unless your will specifically references the pending birth of the child, the law presumes the child was inadvertently omitted and awards that child an *intestate* share of your estate if you die without making a new will. If you make a will and subsequently marry but your will doesn't state that it was made in contemplation of marriage, your spouse will receive an *intestate* share of your estate if you die without writing a new will. And, under the law of many states, if you leave a will in which your spouse receives less than one-third of your probate estate, the spouse is entitled to elect a one-third share of the net estate after certain expenses and creditors' claims. In order to secure this share, an election must be filed with the probate court within specific time frames or the election is waived.

The anti-lapse statute provides that if you leave assets to a beneficiary, and that beneficiary dies before you do, unless the will provides otherwise, the share of a closely related predeceased beneficiary goes to his/her heirs and the share of a non-closely related beneficiary passes to your residuary beneficiaries.

Living Trusts

If you created and fully funded a living trust and die, the terms of that trust will declare where your assets will be distributed. Even though the assets contained in a living trust do not go through the probate process, if your state of residence has enacted a form of the Uniform Trust Code, the trustee will have many of the same duties as a personal representative under a will.

QUESTION: *Now that our children are self-supporting and I am near retirement, my wife and I recently began to review our assets and to use the Internet to gather information to help us plan. It seems that the more information we found, the more confused we have become about what is and what is not in our "marital estate." It has been more than twenty years since we had wills prepared. How can we prepare our wills to take into consideration future growth as it appears we may end up with a taxable estate?*

ANSWER: It appears that your confusion is based on "information overload," which is common in today's complicated world. While self-education is certainly important, it can be dangerous if you are not guided by a lawyer who is qualified in these areas.

Generally speaking, the word "estate" is thought to mean what is left when you die; however, "estate" can mean different things to different people based on their situations. For example:

"Marital estate" is the property that was acquired during a marriage that is divided at the time of divorce based on the law of the state in which the divorcing couple resides. It does not appear that this applies to you.

"Probate estate" refers to the assets that are listed with the probate court after the death of an individual and that pass by will—or by what is called "*intestate* succession" if there is no will. The court retains control of the assets until the debts are paid and then distributes the assets to the beneficiaries or heirs. Generally speaking, pensions and insurance pass outside the probate estate to the designated beneficiaries.

"Taxable estate" is not necessarily the same as probate estate because it includes other assets that are subject to state or federal estate taxes—sometimes called "death taxes" or "inheritance taxes." This means that even though pensions and insurance may not be part of the probate estate, they will be considered part of your taxable estate, if you have not made proper planning.

Through the planning process, which should be accomplished only with the assistance of qualified professionals, you can remove assets from your taxable and probate estates and save estate taxes. So, when you plan your estate, you should look at both (1) the amount in your taxable estate at present and (2) the potential tax on your estate in the future.

One way to estimate the potential size of your estate in the future is to use the "rule of 72s" to establish a "growth pattern." Here's how it works: If your assets are projected to grow at a compounded rate of 8 percent per year, by dividing eight into 72, you will learn that your estate will double in nine years. If your assets are growing at the rate of 6 percent, it will take 12 years for your estate to double.

For federal estate tax purposes, your "taxable estate" will include (1) all interests in property that you own in your name, and all property in a trust you control either directly or indirectly; (2) the proceeds of qualified retirement plans—including 401(k)s and IRAs, with certain exceptions. It is important to remember that in addition to estate tax, qualified retirement plans can also be subject to income taxes because of what is called "income with respect to the decedent" or IRD; and (3) the proceeds of life insurance policies if you either own the policy or the proceeds are payable to your estate.

If you want to keep property out of your estate for tax purposes, you must give up both control over the asset and the right to receive benefits from the asset. Except for certain lifetime gifts, all transfers of money or property you make either during your life or at death are subject to what is called a Unified Gift and Estate Tax System that gives each person a lifetime shelter against federal gift and estate taxes—a sort of "deductible."

Because illness or disability or the need for long-term care can decimate the best estate plan, you should coordinate long-term care planning in order to meet this contingency should it occur.

Section III:
Implementing Your Plan Should You or a Spouse Become Chronically Ill or Incapacitated

6

Health-Care Planning

As we get older, written health-care planning becomes more and
more important. The infamous Terry Schiavo case, where, for many
years, a brain-dead woman in Florida was not allowed to die because she had signed no advance directives, is a case in point. As
part of the planning process, everyone should have the following
necessary health-care documents:

Living Will

A living will (sometimes called a "declaration of a desire for natural
death") is a written statement whereby an individual gives directions
to the physician and family as to what should happen near the end
of life with respect to withholding or providing medical treatment
if he/she has a terminal condition or is persistently vegetative (or
permanently unconscious) and unable to express his/her own wishes for care. A "terminal condition" generally means "an incurable
or irreversible condition that, within reasonable medical judgment,
could cause death within a reasonably short period of time if life-
sustaining procedures are not used." "Permanent unconsciousness"
means the person is "in a persistent vegetative state or has only
some involuntary vegetative or primitive reflex functions controlled
by the brain stem."

The individual must elect in the living will whether artificial nutrition and hydration are to be withheld. If no election is made, these treatments will be provided. The living will allows the individual to give binding instructions directly to the health-care providers, and it is also useful in sparing family members the difficulty of making the choice to withhold or withdraw life-sustaining treatment. However, this instrument has no effect if the medical situations don't involve a terminal condition or a state of permanent unconsciousness.

Health Care Power of Attorney

A more modern, more flexible, and less understood planning document is the "durable health care power of attorney" (health care power of attorney)—also called a health-care proxy. While general powers of attorney have been in use for some time, the health care power of attorney is a relatively recent innovation that arose in the wake of the "right to die" debate. Following the U.S. Supreme Court's decision in the much-publicized Nancy Cruzan case, attention was drawn to the inflexibility of most state statutes with respect to advanced health-care planning. For example, the typical living will statutes enacted by most states only deal with consent to, or refusal of, treatment in very limited circumstances at the end of life. This issue becomes critically important in the case of an incapacitated or incompetent person who requires medical treatment but is neither terminal nor permanently unconscious. Perhaps he or she has suffered a stroke or has advanced Alzheimer's disease. In response to this inflexibility, the health care power of attorney was developed.

As with the general power of attorney, a health care power of attorney is an instrument whereby the principal appoints someone else to act as his agent in a particular matter or class of matters. In the case of a health care power of attorney, the matters upon which the agent acts are health-care decisions instead of financial issues. When the health care power of attorney is in effect, the agent is placed in the "shoes of the principal" with respect to all health-care decisions. Health-care providers are bound to honor these decisions as if they were the decision of the principal himself.

As with the living will, most states have adopted a statutory form for the health care power of attorney, which includes specific language regarding the wishes of the individual who signs the form, often called "the principal." While some people may choose not to use statutory form health care powers of attorney that have been approved by the legislature of their state, the advantages of the statutory form are twofold:

(1) It provides more certainty for medical professionals who might otherwise feel compelled to question the validity of the health care power of attorney or the agent's authority; and

(2) It makes the health care power of attorney more accessible to a much wider segment of the public since it can be disseminated from various sources and does not require individualized drafting by an attorney.

Although the statutory form provides an "off-the-shelf" product for addressing health-care planning, the nuances of the law, the significance of the elections made on the form, and technical aspects as to how the document is put into practice make some type of professional guidance and explanation advisable for most people who sign these documents.

The health care power of attorney is a "durable" power of attorney because the period of the principal's incapacity is obviously the time when the power is most needed. It basically creates a "springing" power that is effective *only* during the principal's incapacity.

The primary strength of the health care power of attorney is the flexibility it provides in designating an individual to make decisions based upon the particular circumstances presented by the principal's condition. The form also allows the principal to give the agent specific instructions with respect to life-sustaining treatments. For individuals who have both a health care power of attorney and a living will, you must look at the law of your state to see which takes precedence in any situation to which it is applicable— i.e., those involving a terminal condition or a state of permanent unconsciousness.

As described below, some individuals want an even greater description of what the agent is to do in certain circumstances. Therefore, they may wish to use a "medical directive," which is discussed later in this chapter.

Adult Health-Care Consent Act

If an incapacitated individual does not have a health care power of attorney and a medical decision is necessary, all states and the District of Columbia have a form of an adult health-care consent act that establishes a hierarchy of persons who may make health-care decisions for an individual who is "unable to consent." The right to make decisions under this act presumably would not extend to termination of life or withholding of life-sustaining treatment without evidence of the patient's desires. The problem with not having a signed health care power of attorney is that should there be a dispute among family members, a judge will probably make the ultimate decision, often at a significant monetary cost to the family.

Emergency Services Non-Resuscitation Order

"Do Not Resuscitate" orders allow an individual who has a terminal condition to request (either directly or through an agent) that a health-care provider issue a "do not resuscitate" (DNR) order for emergency services.

This order allows emergency medical services (EMS) personnel to provide only palliative care if they are called to the home of the individual. Palliative care means primarily pain control. For example, cardio-pulmonary resuscitation (CPR) may be withheld if a patient who is covered by an EMS-DNR suffers a heart attack. Unlike other health-care advance directives, such as the living will and the health care power of attorney, an EMS-DNR may *not* be executed by the individual. It *must* be issued by a health-care provider—generally the treating physician.

Medical Directive

A medical directive expresses, and stands for, the Principal's wishes regarding medical treatments in the event that illness does not allow the Principal to make or communicate directly his or her choices for medical care. Generally, the definitions used in medical directives are as follows:

- Cardiopulmonary resuscitation: using drugs and electric shock to keep the heart beating at the point of death; artificial feeding

- Mechanical breathing: breathing by machine

- Artificial nutrition and hydration: providing nutrition and fluids through a tube in the veins, nose, or stomach

- Major surgery: such as removing the gall bladder or part of the intestines

- Kidney dialysis: cleaning the blood by machine or by fluid passing through the belly

- Chemotherapy: using drugs to fight cancer
- Minor surgery: such as removing some tissue from an infected toe
- Invasive diagnostic tests: such as using a flexible tube to look into the stomach
- Blood or blood products: such as giving transfusions
- Antibiotics: using drugs to fight infection
- Simple diagnostic tests: such as performing blood tests or x-rays
- Pain medications: providing them even if they dull consciousness and indirectly shorten one's life.

Medical Directive: Situation A

If the principal is in a coma or a persistent vegetative state or is otherwise unable to communicate, and in the opinion of his or her physician and consulting physicians has no known hope of regaining awareness and higher mental functions no matter what is done, then the directive signed earlier by the principal—when he or she was healthy—should be followed, assuming the medical treatment desired is considered medically reasonable.

Cardiopulmonary Resuscitation

I WANT _____; I WANT TREATMENT TRIED, IF NOT CLEAR IMPROVEMENT, STOP _____;

I AM UNDECIDED _____; I AM UNDECIDED _____;
I DO NOT WANT_____

Mechanical Breathing

I WANT _____; I WANT TREATMENT TRIED, IF NOT CLEAR IMPROVEMENT, STOP _____;

I AM UNDECIDED _____; I AM UNDECIDED _____;
I DO NOT WANT_____

Artificial Nutrition and Hydration

I WANT _____; I WANT TREATMENT TRIED, IF NOT CLEAR IMPROVEMENT, STOP _____;

I AM UNDECIDED _____; I AM UNDECIDED _____;
I DO NOT WANT_____

Major Surgery

I WANT _____; I WANT TREATMENT TRIED, IF NOT CLEAR IMPROVEMENT, STOP _____;

I AM UNDECIDED _____; I AM UNDECIDED _____;
I DO NOT WANT_____

Kidney Dialysis

I WANT _____; I WANT TREATMENT TRIED, IF NOT CLEAR IMPROVEMENT, STOP _____;

I AM UNDECIDED _____; I AM UNDECIDED _____;
I DO NOT WANT_____

Chemotherapy

I WANT _____; I WANT TREATMENT TRIED, IF NOT CLEAR IMPROVEMENT, STOP _____;

I AM UNDECIDED _____; I AM UNDECIDED _____;
I DO NOT WANT_____

Minor Surgery

I WANT _____; I WANT TREATMENT TRIED, IF NOT CLEAR
IMPROVEMENT, STOP _____;

I AM UNDECIDED _____; I AM UNDECIDED _____;
I DO NOT WANT_____

Invasive Diagnostic Tests

I WANT _____; I WANT TREATMENT TRIED, IF NOT CLEAR
IMPROVEMENT, STOP _____;

I AM UNDECIDED _____; I AM UNDECIDED _____;
I DO NOT WANT_____

Blood or Blood Products

I WANT _____; I WANT TREATMENT TRIED, IF NOT CLEAR
IMPROVEMENT, STOP _____;

I AM UNDECIDED _____; I AM UNDECIDED _____;
I DO NOT WANT_____

Antibiotics

I WANT _____; I WANT TREATMENT TRIED, IF NOT CLEAR
IMPROVEMENT, STOP _____;

I AM UNDECIDED _____; I AM UNDECIDED _____;
I DO NOT WANT_____

Simple Diagnostic Tests

I WANT _____; I WANT TREATMENT TRIED, IF NOT CLEAR
IMPROVEMENT, STOP _____;

I AM UNDECIDED _____; I AM UNDECIDED _____;
I DO NOT WANT_____

Pain Medications (even if they dull consciousness and indirectly shorten my life)

I WANT ____; I WANT TREATMENT TRIED, IF NOT CLEAR IMPROVEMENT, STOP _____;

I AM UNDECIDED _____; I AM UNDECIDED _____;
I DO NOT WANT_____

The medical directive examples above may also be applied to the following situations:

Medical Directive: Situation B

If the principal is in a coma or a persistent vegetative state or otherwise unable to communicate, and in the opinion of his or her physician and consulting physicians has a small likelihood of recovering fully, a slightly larger likelihood of surviving with permanent brain damage, and a much larger likelihood of dying, then the principal may wish to medically direct now his or her wishes regarding the use of medical treatment if considered medically reasonable:

Medical Directive: Situation C

If the principal is in a coma, a persistent vegetative state, otherwise unable to communicate, and has brain damage or some brain disease that, in the opinion of his or her physician and chosen consulting medical experts, cannot be reversed and that deprives the principal of recognizing people or speaking understandably, *and also has a terminal illness,* such as incurable cancer, that will likely be the cause of the principal's death, then the principal may wish to medically direct now his or her wishes regarding the use of medical treatment if considered medically reasonable:

Medical Directive: Situation D

If the principal is in a coma, a persistent vegetative state, otherwise unable to communicate, has brain damage or some brain disease that in the opinion of his or her physician and chosen consulting physicians cannot be reversed and that makes principal unable to recognize people or to speak understandably, *but has no terminal illness*, and can live in this condition for a long time, then the principal may wish to medically direct now his or her wishes regarding the use of medical treatment if considered medically reasonable:

QUESTION: *After he fell and broke his hip, my father began a downward spiral that resulted in his admission to a nursing facility. Although physically healthy, he was unable to walk and became confused, but was still competent. Our mother was not able to lift him, and my brother and I live out of state. My mother admitted him to the nursing home. Later, my brother and I were shocked to find a "do not resuscitate" order that Mom had signed.*

My brother and I went to the nursing facility and were told by the administrator that the "DNR" was required of each resident. Our father is nowhere near terminally ill or at death's door. The administrator won't let us remove this from his file. What can we do to straighten this out?

ANSWER: Obviously, the administrator does not know what he/she is talking about. The facility is placing your father at significant risk and itself at significant potential liability.

Accepted by physicians in all 50 states, the "Do Not Resuscitate" order—more commonly known as a "DNR"—is a type of advance health-care directive that, based on the e-mail and letters we receive, seems to be the very misunderstood, by both individuals and facilities.

In its most simple definition, a DNR is a request that your father not be given CPR (cardiopulmonary resuscitation) should his heart stop or should he stop breathing. Without a DNR order, medical personnel must perform CPR under these circumstances. When signed, the DNR order will be put in your father's chart by the facility physician.

Many patients in hospitals and medical centers may have DNR orders, but they are generally the folks who probably would not benefit from CPR—for example, terminal cancer patients, patients with severe infection, and end-stage renal patients who can no longer be helped by dialysis.

While the DNR is a useful tool in some instances, these documents should not be signed casually by unauthorized people just because some nursing home tells you to do so. Since your father appears to have mental capacity, the decision is his, not your mother's. The only times your mother would remotely have this authority would be if your father were incapacitated and unable to express his desires and (1) she was the agent under your father's health care power of attorney or (2) your father had no written health directive under the adult health-care consent act in your state.

While everyone should consider making advance plans about CPR with his/her doctor before becoming unable to make decisions, the manner in which this was handled by the facility is flat wrong. Just because a document is a part of an admissions package does not mean it has to be signed.

We suggest that if you can not talk some sense into the administrator, you report the facility to your state licensing agency and contact the ombudsman's office to rectify what could become a major problem, before it happens.

7

Long-Term Care Issues, Level-of-Care Decisions, and Payment Options

A half-century ago, Americans died at younger ages. We did not see nursing homes and assisted-living facilities on every corner. When a person needed care for a chronic condition, family members generally provided it at home. But times have changed, and without proper planning, long-term care will decimate an estate and potentially leave the "well spouse" next to penniless.

Long-term care planning is the process of preparing for the medical, non-medical, custodial, and housing needs of chronically ill, disabled, or incapacitated individuals who can't function independently at home, but whose level of care requirement is sub-acute (that is, not requiring hospitalization). While the need to plan for long-term care is not limited to the elderly, this group is most often in need of such planning. To be successful, the long-term care plan must be started as early as possible and must address the level of care required, where that care can best be provided, who should provide that care, how the care should be funded, and how to preserve assets for future needs. In addition to the physical and emotional needs of the disabled person, the psychological and economic effects on the community spouse and family members must be considered.

Before developing a long-term care plan, you must understand your options because if and when that plan is implemented, the institutionalized person will be mentally or physically incapacitated to the extent that he or she cannot function, or perhaps live, without assistance from others. The sooner the planning begins, the more options there are available.

First, you should be familiar with the various levels of care:

Acute Care

If your medical needs can only be provided in the hospital, you need acute care. Acute care is rarely a planning option since most people who need hospitalization are there by medical necessity, not because of planning. Generally, the pay sources for acute care for seniors include Medicare, Medicare Part B, and any MediGap coverage. Otherwise, private health coverage can cover these costs. But if insurance coverage of some type is not available, assets will have to be sold to pay for this level of care. In many instances, after acute care, the patient will receive rehabilitation in a step-down unit of the same hospital, in a separate rehabilitation facility, in a nursing home, or at home. Payment for these coverages, to a limited extent, are the same as for acute care.

Nursing Home Care
(Intermediate or Skilled Level of Care)

Intermediate or skilled care is care provided in a traditional nursing home. The individual's physician and medical team make the determination of whether this level of care is needed or desired.

Residential Care or Assisted Living

The level of care below intermediate or skilled nursing home care is residential care. This is care provided in a residential-care or assisted-living facility. In general, if you need this level of care, while you can't stay home alone and without help, you don't yet meet the criteria for skilled or intermediate services. In other words, you need supervision and assistance with your activities of life. Those most commonly needing this level of care are Alzheimer's or dementia patients. The primary difference between a nursing home and a residential-care facility is the absence of nurses. While nursing homes must have nurses constantly on staff, residential care facilities are not required to have nursing staff, although some do.

Home Care

While most seniors want to stay at home should they become incapacitated, home care is generally limited to those who can operate with some degree of independence, who have a family structure that allows them to remain at home, or who can afford to hire sitters who may be required twenty-four hours per day, certified nursing assistants, or others to help with their deficits. While it is possible to get some assistance through various health agencies at home, this may not be enough. In addition, if the person meets certain very strict requirements, Medicare may pay for some nursing-related care at home. An additional method of alleviating some of the burden on family members is using adult day care centers, which can be found in most communities.

Paying for Long-Term Health Care

Now that you are familiar with the various levels of care, how will it be paid for? Funding usually comes from just three sources: private pay (from the individual's assets and income), long-term care insurance, and Medicaid. While Medicare, Medicare supplement (MediGap) insurance, and Veterans Administration benefits may provide some assistance, these sources of coverage are generally limited and short-term. Providing appropriate long-term care presents serious economic and emotional consequences if appropriate planning has not been accomplished. So it's vital to discard the "it won't happen to me" mentality and develop a plan that is sensitive to the financial resources of your family.

If the elder is a widow or widower, the planning process is easier, unless there is a disabled child or an adult child who has provided care for a long period of time. If the elder has a long-term spouse, the planning will most likely be different from that of the person with a second or third spouse.

While wealthier families may develop a plan that uses private pay, long-term care insurance, or a combination of the two, most middle-income families will develop plans that use a combination of private pay and Medicaid. Families with limited resources are generally forced to look solely to Medicaid. With this in mind, let's look at the following more obvious advantages and disadvantages of the different sources of long-term care payment:

Private Pay

The most obvious disadvantage to private pay is that most families can't afford the $5,000 to $8,000 per month to maintain someone in a nursing home. And maintaining that individual at home with around-the-clock supervision costs even more. Expenses like these will quickly exhaust the resources of most elders, especially if they have other financial obligations outside their care, such as a spouse or disabled child. Depending on where you live, assisted-living facilities can cost between $2,500 and $4,500 monthly. While

Medicaid does not generally cover assisted-living expenses, most long-term care insurance policies do, depending on the policy language. The advantage of paying for long-term care privately, if you can afford it, is that you or your family is in charge, and you don't have to worry about complicated federal regulations or insurance requirements. In addition, there are income tax deductions available for payment of this type of care.

Long-Term Care Insurance

Long-term care insurance, a relatively new product in the insurance field, works in a manner similar to life insurance. The policy holder pays monthly or other types of premiums to the insurance company so that, should long-term care become necessary at some point, the company foots the bill to the extent of the policy language. This type of coverage spreads the cost of long-term care over a large segment of the population, thus lowering the cost to those who need long-term care at the expense of those who do not. While comparatively few Americans have purchased long-term-care insurance, this product will undoubtedly become a major player in the long-term care planning of the future. Obviously, the younger you are, the lower the premium; you can further lower the premium by not purchasing certain policy options you may not need. In order to determine how much daily benefit to purchase and for how long, you must first decide how much of your monthly income you are willing to pay for the care of yourself and/or your spouse in the future.

Long-term care insurance does have its disadvantages: Only people in relatively good health can qualify, although if you have a disorder, the company may choose to "rate" you—that is, increase your premium. While it is much less expensive than the cost of a nursing home if you purchase early enough, long-term care insurance is not cheap. Depending on your age and health, the cost could be difficult to afford. In these instances, it may be a good idea to speak to your children and ask them to help fund the premium. Otherwise, should you need long-term care, your assets will probably be liquidated and your estate lessened. Therefore, long-term care insurance is a hedge bet by your children to protect their potential inheritance. The majority of seniors and Boomers don't have long-term care coverage.

Medicare: A Short-Term Fix

Medicare—the federal program that primarily serves individuals age 65 or older (although some disabled individuals may qualify earlier)—and Medicare supplements will generally pay in varying amounts for up to 100 days in a nursing home following a hospital stay of three days or more, so long as the individual needs rehabilitation or skilled nursing services at the time of hospital discharge and continues to make progress. All costs are covered by Medicare for the first twenty days, but after that, Medicare will pay a daily rate after a daily deductible that changes annually. Either the family or the MediGap coverage pays the difference. (MediGap is health insurance sold by private insurance companies to fill in the "gaps" in the original Medicare plan coverage. Individuals can choose from up to twelve different standardized MediGap policies, all of which must follow state and federal laws.)

When Medicare stops paying, so does the MediGap coverage. Medicare is a short-term remedy.

Medicaid

The final method of pay is Medicaid, a cooperative effort between the states and the federal government to provide medical assistance to certain needy individuals. While Medicaid and Medicare are very different, they are often confused with each other. (See Chapter 8 for a detailed comparison of the two programs.) The obvious advantage and attraction of Medicaid is cost. Medicaid will pay the full cost of nursing home care, including the cost of medications and physicians, so long as an individual is eligible for the program. While the Medicaid recipient's estate may have to repay some of the Medicaid benefits received depending on assets after death, the repayment will be at a daily rate lower than private-pay care. And, depending on circumstances and the level of long-term care planning, repayment may be avoidable.

The disadvantages to Medicaid are equally obvious. First, there is a difficult and time-consuming process to apply for and to remain qualified for Medicaid. Second, most people will have to spend or divest themselves of most of their assets before they are eligible for Medicaid. Third, it may be difficult to gain admission to a nursing home with Medicaid as your source of pay. Fourth, the facilities accepting Medicaid may be limited depending on the time of year and other factors. Fifth, some facilities do not accept Medicaid. Finally, while governmental regulations require that Medicaid recipients receive the same care as private-pay residents, Medicaid recipients will not have private rooms in the nursing home, and they must be assessed by state experts as needing either skilled or intermediate care.

Under the stricter Medicaid laws enacted in 2006, a person who makes gifts prior to entering a nursing home, runs out of money, and makes a Medicaid application within five years after the gift, will incur penalties for each gift beginning at the time when the Medicaid application is made and he or she would have otherwise qualified. If, for example, your father gave you $36,000 within five years of the date that he ran out of other money and applied for Medicaid, if the average cost of nursing home care in his state of residence is $6,000 monthly, he would not be eligible to receive Medicaid benefits for six months after running out of money, being in a nursing home, and applying for Medicaid. (A $36,000 gift divided by $6,000 per month equals a six-month delay.)

To the contrary, based on the law as it was prior to 2006, the penalty period began on the date on which the gift was made. Now, however, the penalty period begins to run on the day you apply for and would have otherwise qualified for Medicaid. Gifts to other than spouses and protected persons made before February 8, 2006, are grandfathered under the three-year look-back rules from the date of gift.

Long-Term Care Partnership Programs

Since February 8, 2006, there has been an increase in the number of states that have passed "long-term care partnership programs." These partnership programs basically provide that those folks who have an approved long-term care insurance policy will be able to qualify for Medicaid after they've exhausted their coverage without being required to spend the vast majority of their assets first.

While these "partnership programs" vary from state to state, if a person has a long-term care policy providing for $300,000 in benefits, they will be able to protect $300,000 of their assets after using up the long-term care coverage, and Medicaid will pick up paying for their bills. As of today, the following state legislatures have passed "partnership laws": Arkansas, California, Colorado, Connecticut, Florida, Georgia, Idaho, Indiana, Kansas, Minnesota, Missouri, New York, Nebraska, North Dakota, Ohio, Oklahoma, Oregon, Pennsylvania, South Dakota, Texas, and Virginia. If your state of residence is not listed, we suggest you contact your state representative or senator to see why your state has not passed this type of legislation.

Because the annual cost of nursing home care averages $75,000 nationally, without some help, most people can plan on spending the vast majority of their nest egg covering these costs. In states where, by purchasing long-term care coverage, a person can resolve this problem—assuming the person is insurable and can afford the premium (or the person's children pay the premium to protect their inheritance)—partnership programs represent an outstanding opportunity to protect against future costs.

Because of the new law and these "partnership programs," over the past several years the high daily benefits, short deductible period, 5 percent compound inflation protection, and lifetime benefit long-term care policies that carried high premiums have given way to stripped-down versions of standard long-term care policies that target Baby Boomers who seek to protect their retirement and other assets from ever-increasing long-term costs with lower premium products. These "slimmed down" policies generally provide three-year coverage periods and, instead of 5 percent annual interest increases, set increases that follow the lower-interest Consumer Price Index.

For example, the John Hancock Leading Edge policy currently costs nearly 30 percent less than a standard policy. The Leading Edge policy has a 100-day waiting period before benefits begin. Benefit-period options are three years, five years, and five years tied to another $1 million in coverage if benefits are still needed after expiration of the benefit periods. John Hancock, among others, also offers a shared-benefit policy that could provide several years of coverage to each spouse or a substantially greater amount to one spouse who can't take care of himself/herself.

You should check with an independent long-term care agent to discuss these options. And, for those for whom long-term care coverage is not an option, there are planning opportunities available through competent lawyers.

QUESTION: *I have been reading your column for several months now and have heard you on the radio. I am 67 and my husband is 74, but he refuses to even think about planning for the potential that he or I may require long-term care. He always says that he has never been sick a day in his life. I am especially concerned because he worked during the marriage while I stayed home. In addition to his Social Security, he receives a small pension and has about $75,000 in his name and a $60,000 IRA. I receive only a small Social Security check and have nothing in my name. Our house is paid for, and we are getting by on our income right now, but he refuses to even consider a power of attorney. Is there anything I can do to protect myself?*

ANSWER: You should be concerned. All too often, women like you face retirement years either alone or with much less financial security than the husband. In fact, studies show that women of retirement age face their later years with less income and greater rates of poverty than men. In many situations like yours, a small Social Security check is the only source of income available to women. One study tells us that only 37 percent of women who draw Social Security benefits today do so based solely on their own earnings history, and 74 percent of elderly widows receive benefits based on the earnings of their deceased spouse.

Women today face significant financial challenges in their later years not only because they have less income and retirement benefits, but also because they are expected to live longer. For example, a 65-year-old woman today can expect to live to age 85, while a 65-year-old man has a life expectancy of age 81.

Since you obviously cannot afford long-term care insurance, and given the clear facts we have stated, we cannot understand why your husband of so many years should not be anxious to engage in the minimal planning it will take to protect you.

First and foremost, he should contact a qualified attorney who will prepare for him—and you—a durable financial power of attorney appointing you as his agent to make business decisions should he become incapacitated. This document should contain broad authorization for you to not only make unlimited gifts to yourself, but also to deal with all issues regarding his IRA, including the right to change the beneficiary and accelerate withdrawals, if necessary. This power of attorney should be prepared to fit your specific needs and should not be purchased at a store or from the Internet.

Second, your husband and you should each sign durable health care powers of attorney so that, should one of you become incapacitated, the other will have the authority to make appropriate health-care decisions. And third, you each need simple wills. We mention wills last because, should one of you become incapacitated and need long-term care, if you don't have durable powers of attorney, the probability of having assets to pass by will is relatively small.

TAKING THE NEXTSTEP: Should your husband need long-term care, without a durable power of attorney containing the provisions we have mentioned above, his bank account and IRA may well go up in smoke, leaving you with nothing to live on during the balance of your life. It is a sad state of affairs when a spouse will not take the steps necessary to protect his mate. We hope this information will help you help your husband to make the right decision.

8

Understanding the Basics of Medicaid

The Medicaid program is a cooperative effort between the states and the federal government to provide medical assistance to certain needy individuals. It was created in 1965 under the Social Security Act. The Centers for Medicare and Medicaid Services, or CMS (formerly known as the Health Care Financing Administration, a part of the United States Department of Heath and Human Services), administers the Medicaid program on behalf of the federal government. The states are required to designate a "single state agency" to serve as the primary state administrator for Medicaid, as well as the contact point for CMS.

In order to participate in Medicaid, a state must provide eligibility to specified mandatory categories of individuals. The state must also provide insurance coverage for a certain group of basic medical services. Beyond these minimum requirements, states have a degree of flexibility in expanding eligibility to additional categories of recipients and/or expanding coverage for an enhanced array of services. A basic description of a state's Medicaid program is contained in the "State Plan," which must be approved by CMS. Funding for Medicaid is provided through a combination of federal and state funds, with the ratio of federal to state funds varying from year to year and from state to state.

Medicare vs. Medicaid

As shown below, these two programs are very different, although they are often confused with each other:

Medicare	Medicaid
Primarily serves individuals age 65 or older, although some disabled individuals may qualify earlier.	Primarily serves indigent individuals, with emphasis on pregnant women, children, disabled individuals, and the elderly.
Financial need is not considered.	Regardless of eligibility category, financial need is a major consideration.
Operates much like a private insurance program (e.g., premiums for some coverages, deductibles and co-insurance payments, etc.).	Different in many respects from traditional insurance (e.g., payment in full, etc.).
Federal program with national uniformity.	Joint federal-state program, with many variations from state to state.
Primarily administered by CMS, with the Social Security Administration (SSA) handling eligibility and enrollment, and "fiscal intermediaries" handling claims (e.g., Blue Cross and Blue Shield).	CMS provides federal oversight, but program is primarily administered at the state level.
Funded primarily through payroll taxes.	Financed with state tax dollars and federal matching funds.

Subject to medical necessity requirements and specified limitations, state Medicaid programs cover a broad array of medical services, including the following:

- Inpatient Hospital Services
- Outpatient Hospital Services
- Physician Services
- Inpatient Physician Visits
- Rural Health Clinic Services
- Laboratory and X-ray
- Durable Medical Equipment
- Pharmacy Services
- Nursing Facility Services (skilled and intermediate levels of care)
- Home and Community-Based Services
- Ambulance Transportation
- Medical Transportation
- Vision Care
- Dental Services
- Home Health Services
- Therapy (physical, occupational, speech)
- Inpatient Psychiatric Services (under age 21)
- Mental Health Clinic Services
- Podiatrist Services
- Family Planning Services
- Early and Periodic Screening, Diagnosis, and Treatment Program (EPSDT)
- Case Management
- Family Support Services

Medicaid Eligibility

To qualify for Medicaid, an individual must be a U.S. citizen or a lawfully admitted alien; must be a resident of the state of application; must furnish a Social Security number or must apply for one; must assign rights to medical benefits or support to the state and must cooperate with the state in obtaining benefits; and must also apply for any other benefits to which he or she may be entitled.

In addition, an applicant must fall within either (1) a category of individuals required by federal law to be covered under a state's Medicaid program, or (2) an optional category of individuals that the state has elected to include. An individual who is not within a covered category will not be eligible for Medicaid, regardless of financial circumstances or medical needs.

There are many Medicaid-eligibility categories, too complicated and numerous to be mentioned here, that are tied to the receipt of other benefits. Because Medicaid is a means-tested program, financial criteria are a major aspect of the eligibility process. All categories of eligibility have an income limit. Most also have a resources limit, meaning that if your resources are above a certain level, you may not be eligible.

Income Eligibility

Most income limits are expressed as a monthly limit and are based upon percentages of federally calculated figures, often the Federal Poverty Level (FPL). Limits are usually adjusted annually, and may vary based on the number of residents in a household. Whether or not incoming funds are considered income is determined by referring to the rules of the most closely associated cash assistance program for the eligibility category in question.

The rules governing Medicaid eligibility (as well as eligibility for other programs) do not necessarily define "income" in the same way that the tax code does. For example, any item received in cash or in-kind during a month is evaluated under the applicable income rules, and may potentially be counted as income. The exception is resources that are converted from one form to another during the month are not considered income. Example: Proceeds from the sale of a residence are considered a conversion of a resource from one form (real property) to another (cash), and are not considered income.

For Medicaid purposes, most eligibility categories evaluate gross monthly income. Deductions generally are not allowed for taxes or other expenses, although some programs may disregard some amount of income. Payments are generally considered income in the month in which they are received. If retained into the next month, they become a resource. Example: Mr. Jones receives $1,000 in pension benefits in January, plus an additional $450 in Social Security benefits. Thus, his total countable income for January is $1,450. If he spends only $1,200 in January, the remaining $250 is carried over into February (presumably in a bank account) and becomes a resource for that month. Items that are considered income in a month are not also considered to be resources in that same month.

Resources Eligibility

Resources are generally defined as assets (including real or personal property) that are available to an individual for use for the individual's support and maintenance. For an asset to be considered a resource, the individual generally must have an ownership interest in the asset and must have the legal right to access (spend or convert) the asset. Depending on where you live, if an individual is below the resource limit at any time during the month, he/she may or may not be considered to be resource-eligible for the entire month.

Some assets are automatically excluded as resources, including 1) home property and contiguous land with up to $500,000 equity, subject to some exceptions (such as a spouse or disabled child lawfully residing in the home); 2) household goods and personal effects; 3) one automobile; 4) a burial space; and 5) irrevocable pre-need burial contracts. Many of these exclusions are limited to a value established as "reasonable" by the U.S. Secretary of Health and Human Services. And, like income determinations, what is or is not considered to be a resource is evaluated using the rules of the most closely associated cash assistance program for the eligibility category in question.

Trusts Eligibility

Medicaid has its own special rules for evaluating some types of trusts. Trusts that fall outside the scope of these special rules are evaluated under the rules governing the particular eligibility category at issue.

Trusts created by an individual for his/her own benefit, or created by the individual's spouse or other person or entity (e.g., court) acting on the individual's behalf, are governed by Medicaid's trust rules. This is true regardless of the purpose for which the trust was created, whether or not the trustees have or exercise any discretion, whether there are any restrictions on when or whether distributions may be made, or whether there are any restrictions on the use of the distributions. In simplified terms, these rules provide for the following treatment of these trusts in determining an individual's eligibility for Medicaid:

Revocable trusts: All trust assets are considered available resources.

Irrevocable trusts: If there is *any* circumstance under which payment from the trust could be made to the beneficiary for his/her benefit, then the trust assets from which such payments could be made are considered available resources. To the extent that there are no circumstances under which trust assets may be made available, the placement of those assets into the trust is evaluated under the transfer of assets rule.

Exceptions to the Medicaid trust rules apply to: 1) a special needs trust for a disabled individual under age 65 if, at the individual's death, the state receives all amounts remaining in the trust up to the amount of medical assistance furnished; 2) a trust composed solely of the individual's income (an "income trust"), if, at the individual's death, the state receives all amounts remaining in the trust up to the amount of medical assistance furnished; and 3) a "pooled trust" for a disabled individual.

In the case of these exceptions, only payments actually made from the trust are potentially countable as income to the individual for eligibility purposes. Additionally, the trust assets are not considered to be available resources to the individual, and placing the assets into the trust does not trigger a transfer penalty.

As previously noted, not all trusts are covered by the special Medicaid trust rules, including testamentary trusts and non-grantor trusts (such as a trust created by parents for the benefit of a child if the trust is not funded with assets belonging to the child).

There are other eligibility considerations to be aware of:

Transfers of Assets

Payment for nursing home services and community-based services will be denied to individuals who have disposed of assets for less than fair market value within applicable "look-back" periods. The rule applies to transfers made by the individual, or by anyone acting on his/her behalf or at his/her direction. For purposes of this rule, the term "assets" means resources and/or income.

Transfers occurring *before* February 8, 2006, continue to be governed by the previous transfer of assets rules, while transfers occurring *on or after* February 8, 2006, are subject to the new rules. As a result, there will be a transition period during which both the old rules and the new rules will be applicable.

Individuals to Whom the Transfer of Assets Rules Apply

The transfer rules apply to "institutionalized" individuals, meaning those in nursing homes, in intermediate care facilities for the mentally retarded, and individuals who receive home and community-based services. The transfer of assets rules also impose penalties if the spouse of the institutionalized individual has transferred assets prior to a determination of eligibility.

The Look-Back Period

Old rule: If the transfer for less-than-fair-market value occurred *before* February 8, 2006, the look-back period is thirty-six months. (A longer look-back period of sixty months applies if the transfer involved certain types of trusts.) The look-back period begins on the date of the transfer. From this beginning date, the look-back period extends back in time for the appropriate interval (thirty-six or sixty months). Any transfers for less-than-fair-market value that occurred within this look-back period are subject to the imposition of a penalty. Therefore, if a person made a transfer for less-than-fair-market value and did not make a Medicaid application until the 37th (or 61st, as the case may be) month after the transfer, there will be no penalty. But if another transfer was made during the time period, penalties are possible.

New rule: If the transfer for less-than-fair-market value occurred *on or after* February 8, 2006, the look-back period is sixty months. The difference, however, is that unlike the old rule, the look-back period begins on the date the individual is both in the nursing facility (or receiving home and community-based services) *and* has applied for Medicaid. Therefore, the beginning date of the penalty was changed from the date of the gift to the date on which the individual is both in the nursing home and applies for Medicaid. This is a harsh change in the law that requires additional and more complicated planning.

Length and Imposition of the Penalty Period

The length of the penalty period during which payment for long-term care expenses will be denied depends upon the value of the asset transferred and the state's average private-pay rate for nursing home care at the time of application. The value of the property or funds transferred is divided by the average private-pay rate to determine the number of months of penalty. Thus, the length of the penalty period corresponds to the length of time during which the individual presumably could have paid privately for his/her care by using the assets that were transferred.

In addition, for all transfers occurring *on or after* February 8, 2006, the state may no longer "round down" when calculating penalty periods, making the "no rounding down" rule effective for transactions taking place after the enactment of the new law.

Today, an applicant who gave $200 to his church, or even to his grandchildren for graduation, could be subject to penalty unless each state adopts some *de minimus* rule.

Prior to enactment of the Deficit Reduction Act (DRA), penalty periods began to run in the month of the transfer unless the transfer occurred during a penalty period that was still in effect for a previous transfer. So, for transfers occurring *before* February 8, 2006, the penalty period continues to begin to run in the month of the transfer, unless the transfer occurred during a penalty period that was still in effect for a previous transfer.

Under the terms of the DRA, if a transfer of assets is made *on or after* February 8, 2006, the penalty period begins to run when the individual is: (1) eligible for medical assistance under the State Medicaid Plan; and (2) would otherwise be receiving institutional-level care based on an approved application for such care but for the application of the penalty period; and (3) if this transfer does not occur during any other period of ineligibility.

Generally, no penalty is imposed for the following transfers (but we suggest that you not make any transfers without the advice of a competent attorney):

(1) Of a home to a: (A) spouse, (B) child under age 21 or a blind or disabled child, (C) sibling with equity interest in the home and who lived in the home at least one year before the individual's admission to the institution, or (D) child who lived in the parental home for at least two years before the parent was admitted to the institution and who provided care for the parent, which delayed institutionalization.

(2) Of assets to or from the individual's spouse, or to another "for the sole benefit of" the spouse.

(3) Of assets to a blind or disabled child, or to a trust established "*solely* for the benefit of" such a child.

(4) Of assets to a trust established "*solely* for the benefit of" an individual under age 65 who is disabled.

(5) If the individual can show that he intended to dispose of assets at fair market value or for other consideration. (This exemption covers individuals who inadvertently—rather than

intentionally—don't receive adequate compensation for the transferred assets.)

(6) If the individual can show that the assets were transferred for some reason other than to qualify for Medicaid. (This exemption is construed very narrowly. Individuals who undertake planned divestments of assets are generally presumed to have done so for purposes related to eventually obtaining Medicaid eligibility.)

(7) If the imposition of the penalty would work an undue hardship. (An undue hardship is defined as discharge by the medical facility or denial of home and community-based services that would result in the individual being placed in a life-threatening situation.)

The penalty period applies to certain types of long-term care services, and does not necessarily mean that an individual loses eligibility for Medicaid entirely or at all for others. So be sure to be well-informed about and understand the Medicaid program applied for.

Note that penalties imposed can be reduced or eliminated to the extent that the transferred assets are returned to the individual.

Community Spouse Rules

Enacted as part of the Medicare Catastrophic Coverage Act of 1988 (MCCA), the community spouse provisions are designed to prevent the impoverishment of the spouse who remains in the community when his/her spouse becomes institutionalized.

The income of both spouses is reviewed, although the income of the community spouse is not considered in determining eligibility for the institutionalized spouse. All assets of both spouses are also reviewed, regardless of the origin of the asset (previous marriage, inheritance, etc.) or the manner in which it would be treated with respect to community property laws, etc. Prenuptial agreements are also disregarded. After the non-countable assets are excluded (e.g., home property, household goods, personal belongings, prepaid burial, and one automobile, etc.), in 2009 the community spouse is entitled to retain countable resources valued at not less than $21,912.00 and not more than $109,560.00 (2009 federal government figures) as set by their state of residence. Any remaining resources are deemed to be available to the institutionalized spouse, and these are counted against his/her $2,000 resource limit.

Once eligibility is established for the institutionalized spouse, the spouses are treated as separate.

Medical Requirements

If Medicaid assistance will be sought for nursing home care, the applicant must be assessed by the state's Community Long-Term Care (CLTC), usually a division of the state's Department of Health and Human Services. CLTC will determine whether the applicant meets the state's Level of Care Criteria (LOC) for Medicaid-Sponsored Long-Term Care Services for skilled or intermediate care.

This determination is based on an assessment of the medical services needed by the individual and whether the individual is afflicted with certain listed functional deficits, as defined by the criteria. In order to be classified as needing a "Skilled Level of Care," an individual must need one of twelve identified skilled services and must have one functional deficit. In order to be classified as needing an "Intermediate Level of Care," an individual must need at least one of four identified intermediate services and be afflicted with one functional deficit, *or* be afflicted with two functional deficits.

Examples of Skilled Services

- Daily monitoring/observation and assessment due to an unstable medical condition. This may include overall management and evaluation of a care plan that changes daily or several times a week.

- Administration of medications that require frequent dosage adjustment, regulation, and monitoring.

- Administration of medications and fluids that require frequent dosage adjustment, regulation, and monitoring. (Routine injection(s) scheduled daily or less frequently, such as insulin injection, do not qualify.)

- Special catheter care (e.g., frequent irrigation, irrigation with special medications, frequent catheterizations for specific problems).

- Treatment of extensive decubitus ulcers or other widespread skin disorders. (Important considerations include signs of infection, full thickness tissue loss, or requirement of sterile technique.)

- A single goal-directed rehabilitative service (speech, physical, or occupational therapy) by a therapist five days per week. Combinations of therapies will satisfy this requirement.

- Nasogastric tube or gastrostomy feedings.

- Nasopharyngeal or tracheostomy aspirations or sterile tracheostomy care.

- Administration of medical gases (e.g., oxygen) for the initial phase of condition requiring such treatment, monitoring, and evaluation (generally no longer than two weeks' duration).

Examples of Intermediate Services

- Daily monitoring of a significant medical condition requiring overall care planning in order to maintain optimum health status (the individual should show a documented need that warrants such monitoring).

- Supervision of moderate/severe memory problem manifested by disorientation, bewilderment, and forgetfulness, which requires significant intervention in overall care planning.

- Supervision of moderately impaired cognitive skills manifested by decisions that may reasonably be expected to affect an individual's own safety.

- Supervision of moderate problem behavior manifested by verbal abusiveness, physical abusiveness, or socially inappropriate/disruptive behavior.

Functional Deficits

Although they may vary from state to state, the four functional deficits are as follows:

- Requires extensive assistance (hands-on) with dressing, toileting, and eating, and physical help for bathing (all four must be present, and together, they constitute one deficit).

- Requires extensive assistance (hands-on) with locomotion.

- Requires extensive assistance (hands-on) to transfer.

- Requires frequent bladder incontinence assistance (hands-on), with daily incontinence care or with daily catheter or ostomy care.

Estate Recovery

Under federal legislation passed in August 1993, the federal government mandated that the states begin estate recovery for expenditures of Medicaid dollars, although assistance furnished prior to July 1, 1994, is not subject to estate recovery.

What is estate recovery? As discussed above, certain assets are exempt from consideration in determining Medicaid eligibility for nursing home care. Prior to estate recovery, a nursing home patient could retain exempt assets and pass them to his/her heirs following death. Under the estate recovery legislation, following the death of the nursing home patient, the state makes a claim against the deceased recipient's estate. As with any other creditors of the estate, this action can force the sale of estate assets—the principal residence, in most cases—in order to satisfy the claim. Thus, absent proper planning, Medicaid eligibility may not save family assets from being exhausted by medical costs.

Anyone facing an estate recovery claim should also keep in mind that the Medicaid claim must meet the same filing deadlines and requirements as any other creditor's claim. Medicaid *must* file a claim with the estate; it is not granted an automatic lien against the decedent's property.

State law does provide certain hardship exemptions that may provide relief under specific scenarios. Many of these provisions track the exceptions to the transfer of assets rule. Additional federal protections were provided by Congress for surviving spouses and/ or disabled children residing in a home that is subject to an estate recovery claim.

Because Medicaid is so complicated, and because rules may vary from state to state, we suggest that you always hire a competent elder law attorney before you do anything. And remember: The earlier in the process you seek information, the more options you will have.

QUESTION: *After paying private-pay nursing home rates for two years (nearly $100,000), I finally figured out that if I did not qualify my husband for Medicaid, I would lose everything and be totally dependent on our children. By getting him on Medicaid, I was able to keep my house, a car, some life insurance, and just over $70,000 in cash. And since my only income was Social Security and some small interest payments, I now receive most of my husband's Social Security. But I am still struggling financially. Our two children are concerned about me and want to give me $10,000 each year as gifts. I am afraid that if they give me money and I go over the limits, my husband will lose his Medicaid, and I will be back where I started. How can they help me without disqualifying him?*

ANSWER: According to a federal law passed in 1988, once your husband ("the nursing home spouse") has qualified for Medicaid, you ("the community spouse") are "split off" from him, and your assets are no longer considered available to him. This means that under the current law, you could win the lottery and your assets would not be available to pay for your husband's nursing home care. However, if your income increases, the amount you receive from your husband's Social Security will decrease by that amount. If your children are thinking about helping you in a meaningful way, you should all seek out the services of a qualified attorney who can assist you in preparing and implementing a plan.

QUESTION: *My wife is in a nursing home and is on Medicaid. I have terminal cancer and a life expectancy of six months. I own a house and have nearly $50,000 in cash, which I want to go to my children because if it goes to my wife, she will be disqualified from Medicaid and the assets will be lost. I hired a lawyer to help me with my will, and he told me that under the law of our state, I must leave my wife at least one-third of my assets without exception. Is this correct?*

ANSWER: No. By leaving all of your assets for the benefit of your wife in a "special needs" trust that can be established in your will, you can make sure your wife receives certain benefits during her lifetime without disqualifying her from Medicaid. You would name one of your children as trustee. At your wife's death, the trustee would distribute the remaining assets to your children.

The advantages of this type of trust include (1) the ability to separate trust distributions from your wife's actual income so that she can receive additional benefits without disqualifying her from Medicaid; (2) the assets of the trust will not be subject to payment of medical bills and will not risk your wife's medical coverage; (3) your wife will be able to receive things she may need but which are not covered by governmental programs; and (4) the cost of administration is not great if a child is trustee. On the other hand, (1) the trust must file tax returns and have its own federal identification number; (2) the trustee must be schooled about how to distribute the funds and for what purposes; and (3) the paperwork is complex and an attorney must prepare the documents and advise the trustee thoroughly.

We recommend that all elders consider wills with special needs trusts as part of their planning process. Because of the complexities involved, these trusts should be drafted only by attorneys who are competent in this field of law.

9

Patients' Rights in Nursing Homes and Assisted-Living Facilities

When Congress enacted the Nursing Home Reform Act (NHRA) in 1987, it made sweeping changes to the expectations of the Medicare and Medicaid programs in their purchase of long-term care services. The NHRA also specifically addressed a number of residents' rights issues, and provided protections to all residents of nursing facilities that accept Medicare or Medicaid. In addition, the NHRA required that a review of a facility's compliance with residents' rights be included in the annual standard survey used to determine overall performance and compliance with federal regulations. It also requires facilities to protect and promote the rights of each resident.

Many state legislatures jumped on the reform bandwagon, often extending the scope of protections afforded to residents and expanding the protection to settings other than nursing facilities.

The residents' rights protections typically fall into the following categories:

- General rights
- Admissions policies
- Transfer and discharge rights
- Access and visitation rights.

The "general rights" include such issues as freedom of choice, freedom from restraints, privacy, confidentiality, grievances, participation in resident and family groups and other activities, and accommodation of individual needs. Residents also have the right to examine the results of the facility's annual survey. These rights must be presented to a resident orally and in writing at the time of admission.

Legislation Affecting Residents' Rights

In order to properly address resident rights, a basic understanding of the general laws involved is needed. The following is a brief outline of some of the state and federal laws that may be applicable in a resident-rights issue.

Medicare and Medicaid Statutes/Regulations

Both Medicare and Medicaid contract with nursing facilities to provide services to program recipients. In order to become, and remain, a provider, the facility must meet the requirements for provider participation set forth in the Medicare and Medicaid statutes and regulations. As previously noted, the Nursing Home Reform Act of 1987 substantially amended these Medicare and Medicaid requirements. The basic purpose of the NHRA was to improve the standard of care and quality of life for nursing home residents by strengthening the requirements of Medicaid/Medicare participation, providing a system of intermediate sanctions for violations, revising the survey and certification process for monitoring compliance, and providing a resident "bill of rights."

The provisions of the NHRA apply to all residents of any facility that participates in either the Medicare or Medicaid program, and set high standards for Medicare/Medicaid participation in several important areas:

- Quality of Care: "Each resident must receive, and the facility must provide, the necessary care and services to attain or maintain the highest practicable physical, mental, and psychosocial well-being, in accordance with [a] comprehensive assessment and plan of care."

- "Based on the comprehensive assessment of a resident, the facility must ensure that a resident's abilities in activities of daily living do not diminish unless circumstances of the individual's clinical condition demonstrate that the diminution was unavoidable."

- Quality of Life: "A facility must care for its residents in a manner and in an environment that promotes maintenance or enhancement of each resident's quality of life."

- Resident Rights: "The resident has a right to a dignified existence, self-determination, and communication with and access to outside persons and services inside and outside the facility. A facility must protect and promote the rights of each resident...."

Veterans Administration Legislation

The Veterans Administration (VA) may provide nursing home care for veterans in its own facilities or in private facilities with which it contracts. VA nursing homes and state VA homes may provide services to veterans with or without service-connected disabilities. State veterans homes receive grants from the VA, and non-VA facilities may be reimbursed by the VA for providing nursing home services to veterans if the nursing home maintains VA-approved physical and professional standards. Veterans qualify for coverage of varying duration, primarily depending on whether their disabilities are service-connected.

Hill-Burton Act

Nursing homes that receive federal construction loans, guarantees, and interest subsidies under the Hill-Burton Act must make available a reasonable amount of free services to those unable to pay. A companion condition is community service assurance: a promise to participate in government-sponsored health care payment programs such as Medicare and Medicaid. The refusal by a certified facility to admit Medicare or Medicaid recipients may provide grounds for filing an administrative complaint or a lawsuit.

Older Americans Act

The federal Administration on Aging helps states and communities develop comprehensive and coordinated service systems to serve older individuals through a network of fifty-seven state and territorial Units on Aging, 660 Area Agencies on Aging, and 25,000 service providers. The act requires that each state have a long-term-care ombudsman program to investigate and resolve complaints in long-term-care facilities.

State Law

In all states there is a bill of rights that closely parallels many of the rights enumerated under the federal Nursing Home Reform Act of 1987. Most significantly, the protections of the NHRA apply to all "long-term-care facilities," which it defines as including not only nursing facilities, but also intermediate care facilities (including those for the mentally retarded) and residential care facilities subject to licensure and regulation by each state's Department of Health and Environmental Control. Thus, the protections may extend specifically into many assisted-living settings, since most are licensed as community residential care facilities.

Specific Patient Rights

Note: Because the rights of an incompetent resident revert to and may be exercised by his guardian, conservator, or durable power of attorney, it is most important to have those documents prepared properly and signed correctly.

Admission Rights

For Medicare- or Medicaid-certified nursing facilities, the NHRA created the following restrictions with respect to admission practices:

1. The facility must provide oral and written information about how to apply for Medicaid and Medicare benefits, how to use such benefits, and how to obtain a refund for previous payments covered by benefits.

2. The facility must not require residents or potential residents to waive their rights to benefits under the Medicare or Medicaid program.

3. The facility must not require oral or written assurances that potential residents are not eligible for or will not apply for benefits under the Medicare or Medicaid programs.

4. The facility must not require a third-party guarantee of payment as a condition of admission, to expedite admission, or as a condition of continued stay in the facility.

5. In the case of a Medicaid recipient, the facility must not charge, solicit, accept, or receive—in addition to any amount otherwise required to be paid under the state Medicaid plan—any gift, money, donation, or other consideration as a precondition of admitting or expediting the admission of the individual to the facility or as a requirement for the individual's continued stay in the facility.

6. The facility must provide information concerning the services available, the charges for those services, and the extent to which the charges are covered by Medicare and Medicaid.

Both federal and state laws require that every new resident of a nursing home or other long-term-care facility (or his/her representative) receive information about resident rights at the time of admission.

Transfer and Discharge Rights

For Medicare- or Medicaid-certified nursing facilities, the NHRA created the following resident protections in the area of transfers and discharges:

Limitations on involuntary transfer or discharge: Facilities are prohibited from transferring or discharging a resident against his/her wishes except under specified, limited circumstances. In general, these circumstances are as follows:

a. The transfer or discharge is necessary to meet the resident's welfare and the resident's welfare cannot be met in the facility.

b. The transfer or discharge is appropriate because the resident's health has improved sufficiently that the resident no longer needs the services provided by the facility.

c. The safety of individuals in the facility is endangered.

d. The health of individuals in the facility would otherwise be endangered.

e. The resident has failed, after reasonable and appropriate notice, to pay for (or to have paid under Medicare or Medicaid) a stay at the facility.

f. The facility ceases to operate.

Documentation of basis for action: The basis of the transfer or discharge (except closure of the facility) must be documented in the resident's clinical record. Transfer or discharge based upon the resident's health or medical needs (items [a] and [b], above) must be documented by the resident's physician. Transfer or discharge based on a threat to the health of others (item [d], above) must be documented by a physician.

Notice requirements: Before transferring or discharging a resident, the facility is required to notify the resident and a family member of the resident or his legal representative of the proposed action and the reason for it. This notice must be in writing, and it must be provided in a language and manner that is clearly understandable by the individuals receiving it.

Timing of the notice: As a general rule, the facility must provide thirty (30) days' notice of the transfer or discharge of a resident, but there are some exceptions to this rule. Under urgent circumstances, earlier transfer or discharge for a reason other than nonpayment or the facility ceasing to operate may be possible, but even in these cases, notice must be provided as soon as practicable before the transfer or discharge.

Content of the notice: The notice must provide the reason for the transfer or discharge, the effective date of the proposed action, and the location to which the resident is being transferred or discharged. In addition, the notice must state that the resident has the right to appeal the transfer discharge to the designated state agency, and must include the name, mailing address, and telephone number of the state's long-term-care ombudsman. Additional information may be required for residents with developmental difficulties or mental illness.

Discharge planning: The facility must provide discharge planning and sufficient preparation and orientation to residents to ensure a safe and orderly transfer or discharge from the facility.

Appeals: The NHRA requires state Medicaid agencies to provide a forum for hearing appeals on all transfer and discharge issues arising under the act, regardless of the individual resident's source of payment.

Bed Holds and Readmission: In addition to transfer and discharge protection, Medicaid (but not Medicare) residents also enjoy the right to return to their facility after they have been absent due to hospitalization or therapeutic leave. In other words, the resident's bed must be held open for a certain period of time. If the hospital stay exceeds the bed-hold period and the resident still needs the facility's services, the resident must be given the first available bed in a semi-private room in the facility.

Other Important Resident Rights

While many of the resident rights guaranteed by federal and state law center around admission and transfer/discharge, there are a number of other protected areas of equal importance to the quality of life of the resident. The following is a brief discussion of some— but not all—of those rights:

- **Freedom of Choice**: Residents have certain rights to be involved in decisions affecting their care and who will provide that care:

  a. The right to choose a personal attending physician.

  b. The right to be fully informed in advance about care and treatment.

  c. The right to be fully informed in advance of any changes in the resident's plan of care and treatment.

  d. The right to participate in planning care and treatment.

- **Privacy**: The resident has a right to privacy with regard to accommodations, medical treatment, written and telephone communications, visits, and meetings with family and resident groups. The facility should arrange for adequate privacy when administering treatment. Staff should knock before entering a resident's room. Staff should not discuss a resident's care or treatment with other residents or unauthorized persons.

- **Married Residents**: Married residents must be permitted to share a room, if they so desire, unless some medical reason prevents this arrangement.

- **Confidentiality**: A resident has a right to confidentiality of personal and clinical records.

- **Grievances**: With respect to a resident's complaints, he/she has the following rights:

  a. The right to voice grievances with respect to care or treatment without fear of discrimination or reprisal.

  b. The right to prompt efforts by the facility to resolve the resident's grievances, including those concerning the behavior of other residents.

  c. The right to written information concerning state agencies that can be contacted if grievances cannot be resolved.

- **Accommodation of Needs:** The resident has the right to receive services with reasonable accommodation of individual needs, except where the health and safety of the resident or other residents would be endangered. Although not included in the residents' rights provisions, the standards set for Medicare/Medicaid facilities by the federal requirements for participation underscore the obligation of the facility to provide individualized care, treatment, and attention.

- **Participation in Resident and Family Groups:** The nursing home must protect and promote the right of residents to organize and participate in resident groups, and the right of the resident's family to meet in the facility with families of other residents in the facility. Further, the facility may not interfere with a resident's religious, social, and community activities that do not interfere with the rights of other residents.

- **Access and Visitation:** A nursing facility must permit the following regarding visitation and access to a resident:

  a. Permit immediate access to any resident by any representative of the U.S. Department of Health and Human Services, any representative of the state, the resident's individual physician, the state long-term-care ombudsman, and agencies responsible for the protection and advocacy for individuals with physical or mental disabilities.

  b. Permit immediate access to a resident, subject to the resident's consent, by his or her immediate family or other relatives.

  c. Subject to reasonable restrictions, permit immediate access to the resident by others who are visiting with the resident's consent.

- **Equal Access to Quality Care:** A Medicaid nursing facility must establish and maintain identical policies and practices regarding the transfer, discharge, and provision of services required under the state plan for all individuals regardless of source of payment.

- **Right to Inspect Survey Results:** A Medicare/Medicaid nursing facility must protect and promote the right of a resident to examine, upon reasonable request, the results of the most recent survey of the facility conducted by a federal or state agency having jurisdiction over the facility.

- **Personal Funds:** With respect to a resident's personal funds, the following conditions apply:

  a. A long-term-care facility may not require the resident to deposit his personal funds with the facility.

  b. If a Medicare/Medicaid nursing facility accepts control of a resident's funds, it must comply with the following requirements:

    (i) Deposit any personal funds in excess of $50 in an interest-bearing account for the resident's benefit.

    (ii) Maintain a full written accounting of each resident's personal funds, including any transactions with those funds, and provide access to such records by the resident.

    (iii) Notify residents receiving Medicaid benefits when the amount in their account reaches $200 less than the applicable resource limit and advise the resident that if the amount in the account reaches the resource limit, the resident may lose Medicaid eligibility.

    (iv) Upon the death of a resident, promptly convey all funds to the personal representative of his estate.

- **Freedom from Abuse and Restraints:** Each resident has the right to be free from physical or mental abuse, corporal punishment, involuntary seclusion, and any physical or chemical restraints imposed for purposes of discipline or convenience and not required to treat the resident's symptoms.

  Physical restraints can be used only to ensure the physical safety of the resident or other residents, and these must be prescribed by a physician. The order must specify how long and under what circumstances the restraints are to be used.

  Psychopharmacologic drugs (drugs that have an altering effect on the mind) can be administered only on the order of a physician as a part of a written drug plan of the resident receiving such drugs.

QUESTION: *My mother was admitted to a nursing home after ten days in the hospital. Although she has been there for a week, we don't think she is getting the services that were ordered by her doctor. We have not been able to get anyone's attention, and Mom is not getting any better. What can we do?*

ANSWER: A person who enters a facility should not get worse just because he or she is in a nursing home. Yet, at the same time, as a concerned family member, you may be expecting too much, too soon. Federal law requires that facilities provide the services and care necessary for each resident to reach and maintain the best mental, psycho-social, and physical well-being possible. Upon admission, each resident receives a comprehensive assessment from an interdisciplinary team of professionals that includes the attending physician, a registered nurse responsible for the resident's care, and other staff personnel who are chosen based upon the resident's needs. Then, within seven days, the facility must develop and implement a comprehensive care plan for that resident. This plan must include not only objectives, but also deadlines for meeting the identified mental, psychosocial, nursing, and medical needs of the resident. To the extent possible, your mother, her family, or other responsible persons should be included in this process.

In addition, the facility must review and revise its plan after each assessment, and all services provided must meet professional quality standards in order to make sure that the resident's activities of daily living (ADLs) do not diminish—unless as a result of the resident's clinical condition that can't be avoided. While you want to assure the best care possible for your mother, you want to try to resolve issues such as this without third-party intervention. We suggest that your first step should be to set a meeting with the administrator of the facility so you can voice your concerns. If you are still not satisfied, you may wish to contact your state ombudsman's office. In order to avoid confusion and confrontations, we recommend that private geriatric care managers become involved in the discharge and admissions process.

QUESTION: *My father has been in a nursing home for the past year, during which time he was in and out of the hospital. Until his money ran out, he was on private pay, and now he is on Medicaid. The nursing home is now telling us that they can't hold his bed while he is in the hospital. What are we supposed to do?*

ANSWER: Since your father is a Medicaid patient, the nursing home is required by law to provide him, a family member, or a responsible party with information that clearly specifies (1) the bed-hold policy under the plan of that state, if any, during which the resident is allowed to return and resume residence; and (2) the facility's policies regarding bed-hold periods that allow a resident to return. Each nursing facility is required by law to establish and follow written policies dealing with bed-hold and what happens if the resident's absence from the facility exceeds the bed-hold period under the state plan. Generally speaking, that person must be readmitted to the facility immediately (if a bed exists) or at the time the first bed in a semi-private room is available. If you did not receive these notices, because of the complexities involved, we suggest you contact an elder law attorney in your area.

SECTION IV:
Other Considerations

10

Divorce—Especially When You're Older

Divorce, second marriages, and cohabitation all require extensive planning, particularly if folks in these situations are middle-aged or older. In this chapter, we look at divorce, especially when you're older. Then, in the next three chapters, we'll discuss what you need to know about divorce at any age, plus the ramifications—financial and otherwise—of second marriages and cohabitation.

Health and Medical Issues

Although children often are not involved, older Americans face much more difficult questions than the younger population before, during, and after divorce, especially when it comes to the impact that divorce has on health and medical issues.

More often than not, private health insurance is provided through employer-sponsored benefit plans. Individuals not covered by group or employer-sponsored plans may try to get personal coverage through the individual policy market, but often it is unaffordable or not available. Important questions on this subject include what your monthly premium will be, as well as the deductible amount (how much an individual must pay out of his own pocket before the health-care provider contributes to the coverage) and the co-payment amount (how much an individual must pay per office visit). Additional issues to consider when purchasing private insurance include whether the policy has certain exclusions for procedures or health issues that may not be covered.

Typically, there is a maximum amount that the policy will cover, and when choosing between different policies, care should be given when considering prospective health-care needs. Further information regarding private health insurance is available from the American Association of Retired Persons (AARP), which can be reached at **www.aarp.org**.

COBRA

If private health insurance is unaffordable or unavailable, divorcing couples can investigate the temporary coverage afforded by COBRA. The Consolidated Omnibus Budget Reconciliation Act (or "COBRA") protects individuals covered by group health insurance and is designed to provide a continuation of coverage where there is a change in circumstances or "qualifying event." The U.S. Department of Labor gives an overview of COBRA:

> The Consolidated Omnibus Budget Reconciliation Act (COBRA) gives workers and their families who lose their health benefits the right to choose to continue group health benefits provided by their group health plan for limited periods of time under certain circumstances such as voluntary or involuntary job loss, reduction in the hours worked, transition between jobs, death, divorce, and other life events. Qualified individuals may be required to pay the entire premium for coverage up to 102 percent of the cost to the plan.

COBRA generally requires that group health plans sponsored by employers with 20 or more employees in the prior year offer employees and their families the opportunity for a temporary extension of health coverage (called continuation coverage) in certain instances where coverage under the plan would otherwise end.[1]

In further outlining who qualifies for continued coverage of group health insurance under COBRA, the U.S. Department of Labor says:

There are three elements to qualifying for COBRA benefits. COBRA establishes specific criteria for plans, qualified beneficiaries, and qualifying events:

Plan Coverage: Group health plans for employers with 20 or more employees on more than 50 percent of its typical business days in the previous calendar year are subject to COBRA. Both full- and part-time employees are counted to determine whether a plan is subject to COBRA. Each part-time employee counts as a fraction of an employee, with the fraction equal to the number of hours that the part-time employee worked divided by the hours an employee must work to be considered full-time.

Qualified Beneficiaries: A qualified beneficiary generally is an individual covered by a group health plan on the day before a qualifying event who is either an employee, the employee's spouse, or an employee's dependent child. In certain cases, a retired employee, the retired employee's spouse, and the retired employee's dependent children may

---

1. The reader is encouraged to visit the U. S. Department of Labor's website at **www.dol.gov** for information regarding COBRA and for information regarding notification requirements in order to continue health insurance coverage.

be qualified beneficiaries. In addition, any child born to or placed for adoption with a covered employee during the period of COBRA coverage is considered a qualified beneficiary. Agents, independent contractors, and directors who participate in the group health plan may also be qualified beneficiaries.

Qualifying Events: Qualifying events are certain events that would cause an individual to lose health coverage. The type of qualifying event will determine who the qualified beneficiaries are and the amount of time that a plan must offer the health coverage to them under COBRA. A plan, at its discretion, may provide longer periods of continuation coverage.

Qualifying Events for Employees:

- Voluntary or involuntary termination of employment for reasons other than gross misconduct
- Reduction in the number of hours of employment

Qualifying Events for Spouses:

- Voluntary or involuntary termination of the covered employee's employment for any reason other than gross misconduct
- Reduction in the hours worked by the covered employee
- Covered employees becoming entitled to Medicare
- Divorce or legal separation of the covered employee

COBRA is not a panacea for everyone, as the length of time for which coverage can be continued is generally limited to eighteen months. In some circumstances, such as divorce or a disability, the continuation benefit may be extended to as much as thirty-six months. A plan may also choose to provide a longer continuation period than those mandated by COBRA.

In short, COBRA acts as a way to ensure that individuals and their spouses, in businesses with twenty or more employees, are provided with continued group health insurance coverage for a finite period during times of change, including job loss and divorce. However, it is important to note that there are specific notice and time requirements with respect to when a beneficiary or spouse must be given notice of the qualifying event and what constitutes a qualifying event.

With respect to divorce, the U.S. Department of Labor says:

> Under COBRA, participants, covered spouses and dependent children may continue their plan coverage for a limited time when they would otherwise lose coverage due to a particular event, such as divorce (or legal separation). A covered employee's spouse who would lose coverage due to a divorce may elect continuation coverage under the plan for a maximum of 36 months. A qualified beneficiary must notify the plan administrator of a qualifying event within 60 days after divorce or legal separation. After being notified of a divorce, the plan administrator must give notice, generally within 14 days, to the qualified beneficiary of the right to elect COBRA continuation coverage.
>
> Divorced spouses may call their plan administrator or the EBSA toll-free number, 1.866.444.EBSA (3272) if they have questions about COBRA continuation coverage or their rights under ERISA.[2]

Because continuation of benefits under a COBRA election generally results in the insured having to pay the entire premium for the full cost of the plan without any assistance from the employer,

---

2. See **www.dol.gov/ebsa/faqs/faq_consumer_cobra.html**.

that individual's ability to pay those premiums may be an issue that merits significant consideration in structuring the financial terms of a divorce settlement. Due to the complex nature of divorces, and the individualized nature of group health insurance plans, the reader is strongly encouraged to consult with a qualified professional for advice as to the effect a divorce will have on continued group health insurance benefits under a specific plan.

Medicare

Older or disabled adults going through a divorce also need to know about health care coverage under Medicare. In its publication *Medicare and You*, the U.S. Department of Health and Human Services provides that "Medicare is health insurance for people age 65 or older, under age 65 with certain disabilities, and any age with End-Stage Renal Disease (permanent kidney failure requiring dialysis or a kidney transplant)."[3]

Medicare falls into four basic categories:

- **Medicare Part A**, which covers inpatient medical care, treatment at skilled nursing facilities, hospice, and home health care if you meet certain conditions;

- **Medicare Part B**, which covers medically necessary services like doctors' services and some preventative services;

---

3. The reader is encouraged to visit the U.S. Department of Health and Human Services website at **www.medicare.gov** where a copy of *Medicare and You* can be viewed in .pdf format. A copy of *Medicare and You* can also be ordered by calling 1-800-633-4227.

- **Medicare Part C** (aka "Medicare Advantage"), which is essentially Medicare's version of an HMO, covering Part A and Part B services (but often with different co-insurance, co-payments, and deductibles), as well as often including some version of Part D drug coverage; and

- **Medicare Part D**, which helps to cover the cost of prescription drugs.

Although Medicare is not a means-tested program that considers income or assets, an individual generally must have accumulated enough work credits to qualify, or be the spouse or a widow(er) of someone who has. Thus, the marriage often plays an important role in determining whether a person—particularly a "stay-at-home" spouse—is entitled to Medicare coverage. Fortunately, when the couple divorces, a spouse who cannot qualify for Medicare on his or her own work record will not necessarily lose entitlement to Medicare based on the marriage.

A person aged 65 or older may be eligible for Medicare as the divorced spouse of a worker under certain conditions:

- validly married under state law;

- married at least 10 years before the divorce was final;

- unmarried, or if remarried, did so after reaching age 60; *and*

- not entitled to monthly Social Security retirement or disability benefits on his or her own record that are greater than one-half those benefits payable on the account of the former spouse.

The worker's spouse must be at least age 62 but does not need to be entitled to Social Security retirement benefits if the couple has been divorced at least two years. Even if the divorced "worker spouse" has died, the surviving divorced spouse may also be entitled to Medicare coverage at age 65 or older (or age 50 if disabled) under certain specific conditions:

- validly married under state law;

- married for at least 10 years before the divorce was final;

- unmarried, or if remarried, did so after age 60 (or after age 50 if disabled) and after the "worker spouse's" death; *and*

- not entitled to Social Security retirement benefits greater than those benefits s/he would receive on the record of the deceased former spouse.

Because income and assets do not factor into eligibility for Medicare, there are generally no significant Medicare issues in structuring the financial terms of a divorce settlement. However, the requirement for a marriage of at least 10 years may lead an individual who is close to this anniversary to consider postponing the final decree until after the 10 years has been achieved, thereby providing the "non-worker" divorced spouse the opportunity to apply at a later date for Social Security benefits on the record of the "worker spouse."

Then, there is Medicaid, which low-income adults going through a divorce may be eligible for:

Medicaid

The U.S. Department of Health and Human Services Centers for Medicare and Medicaid Services provides an overview of who and what is covered by Medicaid:

Medicaid is available only to certain low-income individuals and families who fit into an eligibility group that is recognized by federal and state law. Medicaid does not pay money to you; instead, it sends payments directly to your healthcare providers. Depending on your state's rules, you may also be asked to pay a small part of the cost (co-payment) for some medical services.

Medicaid is a state-administered program, and each state sets its own guidelines regarding eligibility and services.

Many groups of people are covered by Medicaid. Even within these groups, though, certain requirements must be met.

For specific information about enrolling in Medicaid, eligibility, coverage and services for your State, please contact your local Medicaid office.[4]

With respect to someone going through a divorce, the important thing to remember about Medicaid is that qualification does consider income and resources. As a result, financial terms of a divorce can significantly impact an individual's eligibility for benefits. In negotiating divorce settlements, the income and asset levels for various categories for Medicaid coverage may be a significant consideration—particularly with respect to long-term care needs, such as nursing home care.

In some cases, an individual who was able to qualify for Medicaid while part of a couple may find himself or herself suddenly ineligible as the result of having to meet the lower income and resource limits applicable to an individual. Likewise, an individual who experiences a decrease in income or assets as the result of a divorce may become eligible for the first time.

In attempting to qualify for Medicaid, excess assets can generally be "spent down" through the purchase of legitimate goods or

---

4. The reader is encouraged to visit the U.S. Department of Health and Human Services Centers for Medicare and Medicaid Services website at **www.cms. hhs.gov** or contact their own state Medicaid provider or health department for further information about Medicaid eligibility and benefits. Contact information for state health departments can generally be found in the government section of your local phone book or by visiting **www.cms.hhs.gov/ContactCMS/**.

services needed by the individual or converted into other assets that do not "count" for Medicaid eligibility purposes.[5] However, having income that exceeds the Medicaid eligibility limit may be more problematic. Therefore, in structuring a divorce settlement, it may be more advantageous in some circumstances to take a lesser amount of spousal support in order to be able to remain below a Medicaid income limit if and when the need arises. In such a case, the lower alimony could be counter-balanced by a larger slice of the pie when the marital assets are divided. The nature of the assets a party receives may also be a consideration, as some assets are "excluded" in the Medicaid eligibility determination while others are "counted."

A party may also want to consider a higher share of the marital assets in exchange for a lower support payment if there is concern that the paying spouse may be destined for nursing home care and Medicaid eligibility. Because Medicaid is not a party to the divorce, it will not feel constrained by the terms of the divorce and may not easily recognize the supporting spouse's obligation to make alimony payments (preferring instead to have that supporting spouse channel all of his or her recurring income toward the cost of his or her care, thereby reducing Medicaid's payment obligation).

A savvy settlement negotiator may include some provision for securing the future support payments with specific assets of the paying spouse, or for providing a means of allowing the termination of future payments upon the conveyance of certain assets to the payee spouse.

When conducting asset preservation planning in the context of Medicaid eligibility and long-term care needs, couples often have

---

5. For example a primary residence, an automobile, and pre-need funeral contracts, among others.

decidedly more flexibility than single individuals, due in large measure to the fact that spouses can freely transfer assets back and forth between themselves without triggering Medicaid eligibility penalties. A divorce will result in the loss of much of this flexibility. As a result, an impending nursing home admission for one spouse in a couple that is contemplating a divorce may require some pre-divorce measures to maximize the planning opportunities that may ultimately benefit both members of the couple—and potentially their respective progeny.

Again, due to the complex nature of divorces and because Medicaid eligibility requirements can vary greatly from state to state, the reader is strongly encouraged to consult with a qualified professional for advice as to the effect a divorce will have on the present and future availability of such benefits.

Financial Issues

Although most people tend to believe that divorce happens when people fall out of love or can't get along, that is not always the case. Sometimes folks who love each other are forced into divorce because of financial considerations. Indeed, the pursuit of financial devastation was never in the marriage vows, but more and more couples now are headed down that road because, today, staying married sometimes means a plunge into economic ruin.

In an uncertain economy, seniors are being required to revisit their retirement plans. And when one spouse becomes chronically ill, the impact of the cost of care on even the best-laid retirement plan can be disastrous. According to the U.S. Department of Medicare and Medicaid Services, more that 40 percent of people over age 65 are expected to spend some time in a nursing home. While most won't stay long—more than half of nursing-home stays last six months or less—the price can still be staggering: an average of more than $5,000 a month for a semiprivate room, according to a MetLife survey. And, 10 percent of those seniors admitted to a nursing facility will stay for five years or more.

This fact, coupled with restrictive laws enacted in February 2006 to target Medicaid planning, will snare more and more unsuspecting seniors, their families, and the nursing homes that care for them. These restrictive changes can penalize seniors by disqualifying those who make church contributions or help a grandchild go to college and later apply for benefits within a five-year look-back period.

Thus, a portion of the increasing number of people over 65 getting divorced today can be traced to financial considerations. For example, when one spouse is in a nursing home, divorce may be the only option in order to preserve assets for the future support of the healthy spouse. This is because Medicaid's draconian guidelines demand near-exhaustion of a couple's assets before a spouse in a nursing home will qualify for benefits.

Aside from a residence valued at less than $500,000 (or $750,000 in some states) and some other non-countable resources such as an irrevocable prepaid burial contract, the Community Spouse Resource Allowance (CSRA) is relatively low. So when one spouse becomes chronically ill, more couples are coming to the realization that spending most of their assets to pay for nursing home care will leave the healthy spouse without sufficient resources to live.

The federal Medicaid program establishes what assets are "countable" for eligibility purposes, and which are ignored because they are "non-countable." At the time a Medicaid application is made, the spouse in the nursing home can own only $2,000 in countable assets.

Examples of countable resources—that is, assets you can sell and withdraw even if you are assessed penalties and taxes—include cash, money in banks (joint accounts with others are presumed to belong to the applicant), trusts, deferred annuities, stocks, securities, bonds, cash-surrender value of life insurance, 401(k)s and IRAs (depending upon where you live), and pensions and annuities in pay status to the extent you have withdrawal rights other than a monthly payment.

Once divorced, the spousal resource rules no longer apply, and the assets allocated to the spouse not in the nursing home don't count. However, since Medicaid probably won't recognize payments of alimony by a nursing home spouse to a community spouse, efforts should be made to shift more assets to the community spouse in order to make up for the support he or she will not receive in the future.

Other important things to remember include:

- Both matrimonial and elder law attorneys should collaborate to create a plan before the divorce is final, because until there is a divorce, without an appropriate will, the assets held by the community spouse could well pass to the nursing home spouse in whole or in part.

- Before a divorce, estate planning documents should be signed to minimize the potential of the nursing home spouse receiving the assets directly while complying with state law. This includes changing beneficiaries on life insurance policies, IRAs, annuities, and other assets. In most situations, changing the beneficiary of a 401(k) requires spousal consent, but this is not true for IRAs.

- Joint accounts should be modified to remove the nursing home spouse as a title owner where possible, and if a trust is in place, restatement and amendment of the trust beneficiaries is essential. In some cases, the community spouse may want to create a special needs trust for the nursing home spouse to make sure non-Medicaid expenses can be covered. These are specialized trusts that should only be created by qualified attorneys.

- Because divorce terminates the husband-and-wife relationship, if the community spouse desires to remain in control of the nursing home spouse's health-care decisions when appropriate, the nursing home spouse should sign a health care power of attorney or proxy that names the community spouse as agent to make the health decisions should the nursing home spouse be unable to do so. This document could also allow the community spouse to continue to visit the nursing home spouse. At the same time, the community spouse should change his/her health-care proxy from the nursing home spouse to another family member or trusted individual.

- Similarly, the financial durable power of attorney should be changed by the community spouse to remove the nursing home spouse from a position of making decisions. This is needed, for example, because if the nursing home spouse retains the right to make gifts of the community spouse's property, those resources will be deemed available by Medicaid.

- While some people question the ethics of divorcing a spouse who will require long-term care, protection of economic security is essential. Most couples in long-term marriages are concerned about each other's welfare, and if divorce can save assets for the well spouse while providing the chronically ill spouse the same quality of care at a much more reasonable cost, the decision to divorce may be the only one the couple can make.

- While some believe it is unethical to take advantage of the legalities that are available to qualify a spouse for Medicaid, those same people take tax deductions for charitable contributions, write off casualty losses, and deduct interest and taxes paid on the homes to reduce their tax bills.

Question: *My husband and I are 62. I have never worked outside the home. After 42 years of marriage, he has suddenly decided that he wants a divorce. I am devastated. What do I need to know to protect myself as this separation and divorce moves forward?*

Answer: There are special health and financial issues that older people need to know about as they are preparing to divorce. Your attorney should be able to help you understand and prepare for these issues, but here are several things that you and other seniors should especially be aware of as they go through the divorce process:

- Usually, private health insurance is provided through employer-sponsored benefit plans. If you cannot continue to be covered under your husband's health insurance policy, you need to ensure that you retain some kind of health insurance until you are 65 and will probably qualify for Medicare. This could be temporary coverage afforded by COBRA (the Consolidated Omnibus Budget Reconciliation Act) designed to provide a continuation of coverage where there is a change in circumstances or a "qualifying event" such as divorce. COBRA, however, is expensive.

- To qualify for Medicare once you turn 65, you generally must have accumulated enough work credits to qualify, or be the spouse or widow(er) of someone who has. There are specific conditions under which you, as a stay-at-home spouse, could qualify for Medicare as the divorced spouse of a worker. Make sure that your lawyer explains these conditions to you so that you can determine if you will be eligible for Medicare in three years.

- Financial terms of your divorce can significantly impact your eligibility for Medicaid benefits, if you ever need them. A good lawyer can help structure a settlement that will allow future availability of Medicaid to you should you ever need it.

- Before divorcing, beneficiaries on life insurance policies, IRAs, annuities, and other assets should be changed. This is especially important to an older couple that has accumulated a lot of assets.

- Before divorcing, estate planning documents should be signed to ensure that you will not be responsible for any medical or nursing home care that your husband might need in the future.

11

Divorce—What You Need to Know at Any Age

At the time of separation and divorce, support systems are important. But it's difficult to find people who understand what you are going through and who, like you, want information and someone to talk to confidentially. Knowing the questions to ask is much more important than knowing all of the answers. Practical, objective information can start you out on the right foot and provide a better quality of life after divorce.

So, if you are separated, divorced, or just thinking about it, we will give you a road map, a practical way for you to learn to deal with the process, ask the right questions, and gain control of your life. Here is a short list of what to keep in mind:

- Panic and emotions have no place in the decision-making process. Understand your options, channel your energies, and then make informed decisions.

- The advice of friends and family will confuse you. If those who have "been through it" want to help you, ask them just one question: "If you had it to do over again, what would you do differently?"

- Keep your goals in perspective; your lawyer can't do it all for you. You will make a mistake if you allow the lawyer to make your decisions, because if you lose control of your case, you lose control of your life and place yourself at the mercy of an unforgiving court system.

- Try to negotiate as many of the issues as you can after you are informed.

- A negotiated settlement lasts as long as those involved want it to last, so keep your goals in perspective. Ninety-five percent of all divorce cases are settled—many times at the last minute on the courthouse steps—and to no one's satisfaction.

- Fighting for principle, or just to fight, is a bad business decision. Still, although a long-term war may have adverse economic and emotional consequences, that doesn't mean you should give up important rights just to try to get the case over with.

- Never sign an agreement without the advice of a lawyer. And never allow one lawyer to prepare an agreement for both you and your spouse. You always need your own lawyer.

Where to Start?

Here's some advice on how to get started:

- Begin to plan now. Leave nothing to chance because it's very difficult to try to change the economic details of a divorce after it is over.

- Separate your emotions from the practical issues you must face. Get a clear picture of your future needs. Get organized and focus on the important issues.

- Buy a notebook; then put all of your questions and concerns in writing before you meet with your lawyer. Give your lawyer a clear understanding of your needs and goals so that an effective strategy can be planned and your lawyer can concentrate on what's important.

- Write a brief, frank history of your marriage with dates, employment histories, illnesses and disabilities, and other relevant information. Then, objectively document the contributions and sacrifices both you and your spouse have made during the marriage and your concerns for the future.

- Begin preparing your budget. Review your checking account records for the past two years, then categorize and list the deposits and your monthly expenses. Note expenses that may be paid semi-annually or annually, such as property taxes and insurance.

- List all benefits provided as a result of employment—yours and your spouse's—such as pensions, automobiles, health and life insurance plans, etc., especially where there is a closely held business.

- List all assets you know of, including their costs and estimated current values. Use insurance policies covering your home and cars, newspaper ads, stock prices, etc., to get some idea of how to appraise these assets. You must also itemize your debts.

- Just as you should inventory your home and videotape your belongings for insurance purposes, now you should photocopy and photograph every financial record and piece of property. Keep the photocopies and photographs in a safe place, such as a bank safety deposit box.

The more information you take to your lawyer, the better you will understand the process, and the better your chance of success.

Your Lawyer's Role, and Yours

You cannot afford to misunderstand what your lawyer is supposed
to do for you. Your lawyer is not a marriage counselor and should
not be expected to make your personal decisions for you. When
you hire a lawyer, remember that lawyer is working for you to:

- evaluate the facts of your case and the legal issues involved,
  then advise you about your rights and obligations

- advocate your side in all aspects of the process

- negotiate a fair settlement under the circumstances of your case

- provide you with competent referrals concerning the many
  non-legal issues which may arise, such as taxes and appraisals.

Your job is to prepare yourself, to be totally honest with your lawyer, and to provide complete information. If you give incomplete or
bad information, you can bet that you will have bad results.

How do you find a lawyer? First, look for an attorney who is
competent in this area. You may want to interview more than one
lawyer before you make a decision. Find out how much of the lawyer's practice is dedicated to matrimonial work and, if you are older,
to elder law work. Make sure you are comfortable with your lawyer
and the staff members who will be involved in your case. If, for any
reason, you don't feel comfortable, find another lawyer.

Your relationship with your lawyer is one of trust. Anything you
tell your lawyer *one-on-one* is privileged, meaning your lawyer is
duty-bound not to repeat your confidences. The same holds true
for the lawyer's support staff. To maintain this privilege, *don't* bring
others with you when you meet with your lawyer, and *don't* discuss
your case with friends.

You should expect that your lawyer will rely upon experts in such
fields as taxation and valuation so that your case can be effectively

prepared. If he or she doesn't call in these experts, ask why not. Financial and insurance arrangements, in particular, require careful attention. But it is unfair and unrealistic to expect your lawyer, or any one individual, to be an expert on every subject involved to achieve a successful result. So ask about experts who can help you get credit, make investment and insurance decisions, and meet your real estate needs.

Don't expect definite, precise answers to all of your questions. Lawyers' opinions are generally based upon ranges of probability which, in turn, are based upon the information you provide. Anything not clearly covered in your divorce papers is probably lost forever. Plan now to try to avoid later misunderstandings due to ambiguities. Ask your lawyer to mail you copies promptly of everything done in your case. Keep a checklist and always be involved in the progress of your case.

Don't be impulsive, and don't call your lawyer constantly. Unless it's an emergency, talk to the administrative assistant first. Always put your questions in writing before you meet with your lawyer, and take a pad and pencil with you to make notes. Don't waste time with small talk and jokes—jokes aren't funny when you are paying for them.

No lawyer should guarantee you a result. If your lawyer suggests that you can do better than what is offered, find out: 1) how long it will take to get a better result; 2) the range of what the "better result" can be; and 3) the cost of getting a better result. Then look at the situation and see if it's worth the time, money, emotional strain, and risk to try to do better.

The court system is simply one way in which disputes are decided. It has a language all its own and may seem complex, but there are rules and time limits. You need not be afraid of it, but you must respect it. Get a basic understanding of how the system operates so you will know what to expect, and when. You may be interested in mediation and arbitration as alternatives to court. Ask your lawyer to explain these options.

If, for any reason, you don't trust your lawyer, don't hold it in. Try to talk it out. If you still aren't satisfied, find another lawyer. Your case can affect the rest of your life. If you want a second opinion, get one. Ask your lawyer where you stand; you're entitled to know. And, although your lawyer cannot guarantee you a result, you are entitled to know the following:

- the range of possible results
- the strong and weak points of your case.
- the worst result you can anticipate based upon the information you have provided
- the average length of time to complete a separation or divorce action in your locale if settled, if litigated in court, and if appealed. And, *always* ask about the cost.

You may be told that some of your goals are unrealistic, that you want too much, or that you are not asking for enough. If your lawyer agrees with everything you say or you get no feedback, be concerned. Never waive important rights just because you want to get finished with the case. At the same time, there is little economic sense in fighting for lost causes. Always compare the chances of achieving your most important goals with the cost in time and money. You should decide which causes you are willing to fight for, and which you are willing to negotiate or give up.

The Family Home

In many instances, the family home may be one of the most significant assets acquired during the marriage. Unless an agreement is made to the contrary, a court may deem it unfair to let one of you use the residence and tie up the other's equity for a long period of time. On the other hand, it may be less expensive for a spouse to remain there. In either case, prepare for the contingencies—not to mention possible tax consequences. Here are some of the considerations you should be aware of about the family home:

- What is the likelihood the family home will be sold? Begin to look into alternative housing for you and any disabled child who may be dependent upon you. Compare the cost and understand the potential tax consequences.

- Get an estimate of how long it will take to sell the house for close to what it's worth. Check on the real estate market in your locale by calling realtors and brokers. Get information, but don't sign anything.

- If there is a move, someone will have to pay for the packing and moving expenses. Get estimates from moving companies and add this expense to your checklist. Then, make sure that your settlement covers this expense.

- If there is a sale, determine how the insurance, tax, and other escrow funds will be divided.

- If you want to try to keep the house, you may want to look into a total refinancing, a second mortgage, an equity line, a home equity loan, a reverse mortgage if you are over age 62, or another means by which one of you can buy out the other's share. If you don't have credit or the financial means yourself, consider asking relatives who may be willing to help you buy out your spouse.

- Disputes over furniture and personal property can be expensive. Think about how to fairly evaluate and divide personal property. Be reasonable. In many cases, people get carried away with emotions and pay lawyers more to fight over personal property than it would cost to replace the property.

- If you are planning to buy another home, shop for mortgages. Remember that in addition to the down payment, you will need enough money to pay fees, insurance, property taxes, title insurance, and various closing costs. And, make sure to find out what price home you will need to buy in order to defer tax consequences.

Auto and Homeowners Insurance

The last thing you want to do is cancel any insurance. All parties and all assets should remain covered for everyone's protection; otherwise a liability claim or casualty loss could wipe out the assets you have accumulated. Both of you need to explore liability and casualty coverage options for the present and future:

- If you or your spouse is planning to leave home, or if one of you has already left, find out if the current automobile insurance covers you. It may be necessary to purchase another policy to protect your assets, so check it out.

- Whoever leaves needs to buy a tenant's insurance policy to cover personal property taken to another residence or apartment. The current homeowners' policy will probably not cover that property.

- If there is a move, the homeowners' policy will not cover perils that may occur during the move. Moving insurance coverage is available and should be considered. And, make sure a policy is in place when the property arrives at its destination.

- Make sure that the limits of coverage and deductibles currently in place will best protect your assets. When new coverage is purchased, the same questions must be asked and answered.

- Rules of thumb: 1) Keep an amount in a savings account equal to your deductibles; and 2) make sure the limits of coverage are sufficient to protect your assets and replace your assets at today's values.

- Valuables (such as furs, jewelry, etc.) must be listed and appraised. You will need a separate policy because these items are not covered by the standard homeowners' policy.

Health Coverage: It's Important to Everyone

Without quality health coverage, the cost of a catastrophic illness or injury can wipe out everything you have worked for. The cost of health care and health insurance is rising, and it's hard to find good coverage. But everyone involved has a vested interest in finding out what you've already got, how to keep it, and how to make sure it's provided for in your settlement. Consider the following:

- More often than not, health insurance is provided through employer-sponsored benefit plans or, in some instances, through military, civil service, or state/municipal governmental health plans. In some states, continuation of coverage is available if a special order is issued at the time of divorce.

- Under certain circumstances, the working spouse's health insurance will provide coverage for the non-working, non-insured spouse for thirty-six months at group rates under the federal law known as COBRA. After thirty-six months, there can be a conversion at higher individual rates.

- Ask the benefits administrator about compliance with important options and elections. Get estimates of the increased costs after three years so you can plan future budgets. Check out all elections that are necessary to continue coverage, and make sure they are made on time. If you have any minor or disabled children, make sure that coverage for them continues.

- Plan for the rising costs of health care and health coverage in your settlement. If you plan now, you should be able to avoid disputes and expenses later. If you are paying support, not having health coverage on dependents may cost you later. If you are receiving support, your budget must include enough to keep up coverage as the rates and deductibles increase.

- If there is a pre-existing condition that might make it difficult for the non-working spouse or minor/disabled children to secure health coverage, examine all options that are available now. New policies often have extended periods of time when pre-existing conditions are not covered, so never cancel any insurance policy until you know what will replace it. And never buy a policy until you know what is covered and when it's covered. Read the policy, and don't rely on a brochure or the representations of an agent.

- If either spouse or one or more children is disabled, there are options ranging from public education to governmental benefits that don't require reimbursement. Scout for these options before you sign any agreement or go to court. A little research may save you both time and money.

- In some employee health plans, term life and disability insurance are included as benefits. If so, check into the beneficiary designation.

- If one spouse was or is in the military, there may be medical benefits for dependents. Call the Judge Advocate's office nearest you. Or, call your U.S. congressman or senator for information. Do it before your case is over.

Other Health-Care Issues

Another issue that often arises during a divorce is who is going to make health-care decisions for you if you become incapacitated before, during, or after the proceedings—times when you certainly don't want your (ex)spouse to be in charge. Generally, a person is able to set out in writing the extent of and what types of care they would like to receive, or whom they would like to be able to make their health-care decisions for them, by way of a living will, a medical power of attorney, or a durable power of attorney (see Chapter 6 for definitions).

Usually, a copy of a living will is given to a trusted family member, often a spouse, and the terms you set out in your living will cannot be overridden by any family member(s). Because a spouse may be in possession of your living will, it is advisable during contentious divorce proceedings to revoke any previously executed living will naming your spouse and to execute a new living will to be left in the possession of another trusted person.

Similarly, during contentious divorce proceedings, it would also be wise to revoke any previously existing medical power of attorney or durable power of attorney naming your spouse, and to execute a new document naming another trusted person.

There is also the issue of your medical records during a divorce. The Health Insurance Portability and Accountability Act (HIPAA) is a federal statute that was enacted for the purpose of regulating the keeping and dissemination of medical records and information. Under this law and under many state laws, individuals are entitled, among other things, to access to their medical records, and to be assured that the information contained in those records will be maintained in a confidential manner. Often, a treating entity, such as a hospital or doctor, may ask you for your consent to make this information available to other individuals if the need arises. This consent or waiver must be in writing, must be signed, and must designate what information can be disclosed, who can disclose it, and to whom it can be disclosed. If you have previously named your spouse as a person who can have access to your medical information, it may be wise in a contentious divorce proceeding to contact your medical providers and inform them that you no longer want your spouse to be given access to your medical information. It also would be advisable to re-execute your consent waiver.

The Basics of Alimony and Support for Disabled Children

There are all kinds of alimony: permanent, periodic, lump sum, temporary, rehabilitative, and reimbursement. Child support for disabled children can continue for so long as the child lives, regardless of age. Each state has laws that govern the application of alimony and support in its court system, so you should always check these things out with your lawyer. But there are some general things you need to know:

- Find out how long each type of payment can last in your state. Remember: planning for employment options and children's education must begin now.

- Always check out the tax consequences of what you are going to pay or receive. It is too late to plan after the agreement or court order is signed. Make sure your lawyer or CPA explains to your satisfaction the tax consequences of all payments.

- "Alimony" as defined by the state may not be "alimony" as defined by the IRS. It may or may not be taxable to the receiving spouse or deductible to the paying spouse, depending on how the agreement or court order is worded.

- Child support is not taxable to the receiving spouse and is not deductible to the paying spouse. There are questions about dependency exemptions and medical expenses, however, which may affect your tax situation. Get informed now so there are no misunderstandings later.

- If the dependent spouse or a child is disabled, there must be planning, not only for education but also for the length of the support obligations. Find out what public benefits may be available, and then structure a settlement around these benefits and ensure that the settlement avoids reimbursement by using special needs trusts.

- If the paying spouse becomes disabled or dies, there should be security so that alimony and support payments can be continued. Although Social Security benefits may be available, these payments may not be sufficient.

- Check into disability insurance and life insurance options. Remember that if you have an insurable interest in the life of the person on whom coverage is sought, you can buy the policy. In this way, Social Security can be supplemented.

- Try to plan for cost-of-living increases. Check out whether your payments can be tied to the Consumer Price Index from the U.S. Department of Labor or other statistical data that can be used to automatically increase (or decrease) payments. Such a provision may save later court appearances.

- Determine if anticipated interest income from the division of assets you get will affect the amounts of support or alimony you pay or are to be paid. If so, you need to know when you will get the money and how to invest the money in a safe fashion so that you get that return.

- Check into special programs for disabled children or dependent adults who need special types of planning available in the public sector. Build the agreement around these benefits.

- Ask all of the same questions to plan for the education of a dependent spouse who needs to become trained to enter or re-enter the work force.

Security for Payments and Obligations Is Essential

- Plan for ways to protect support and alimony awards so that if the supporting spouse dies or becomes disabled, benefits can continue. Use disability and life insurance, or an annuity, or a contract to make a will. Make sure that any obligation is funded with life insurance and disability insurance, because Social Security for children whose parents die terminates at age 18, well before most children enter college. Reach agreement on who will pay for this protection.

- Find out if the obligated spouse can be required to obtain life insurance or long-term disability coverage in case of death or an unexpected inability to work. Then, check into cost and who will be required to pay. If you are the receiving spouse, it may be wise for you to agree to pay the premiums for policies in order to protect what you receive.

- Determine if an existing disability or life insurance policy can be used or whether a new policy is needed. This question is often answered based upon the cost of the policy and the amount of benefits available. Check into anticipated coverage and cost. But remember that governmental and some employee policies should be avoided because of complex rules about beneficiary designations.

- If someone other than you is making the premium payment, make sure that you get regular proof of premium payment and beneficiary designation. If possible, own the policy and pay the premium, because then you don't have to worry about non-performance or having to go back to court to get information.

- Determine who will own the cash values of existing policies and how they can be used. If you are going to make the premium payments on an existing policy that builds cash value, make sure that the cash is not taken out of the policy.

- There may be tax consequences in connection with the transfer of ownership of policies and collection of insurance proceeds. Find out what these consequences are and plan for them now.

- If one spouse is uninsurable, check into alternatives that may be available. Make sure that existing policies are continued, for everyone's protection.

- Always check into the beneficiaries of all policies to make sure that the appropriate persons are designated. Remember: Only the owner of a policy can change the beneficiary.

- Beneficiary designations must be considered closely. Remember that governmental insurance programs preempt state court orders. This means that if the court order requires a beneficiary designation on a federal insurance program, and it is not accomplished, there is nothing you can do. So consider using separate policies and make sure you regularly obtain proof of premium payment and beneficiary.

- Ask about a contract to make a will. Find out what it is and how to enforce it. Whatever the contractual aspects turn out to be, make sure they are clearly spelled out in your settlement.

Don't Overlook Credit and Division of Debt

The importance of credit and debts is often overlooked, but the long-range effects of any settlement must include liability management and planning. The following tips cover a number of issues:

- Always plan by using net figures. For example, if a piece of property is to be sold for $50,000 and you are to receive one-half, remember that your net share will not be $25,000, but $25,000 reduced by the costs of sale, the payment of any mortgage, the payment of taxes, and the payment of lawyers' fees.

- Before the divorce, look into the status of your credit. If you are authorized to use a credit card but are not obligated on the account (which is often the case), you may have no credit history and, therefore, no credit. If an account is used by both of you during the marriage, it does not mean that both of you have credit ratings and credit histories.

- There are ways that credit can be established for someone who has never had credit. You can, for example, go to a bank and take out a small loan (get a relative to endorse your note, if necessary), put the proceeds into a savings account, and repay the loan with interest. Then, use this credit source to open other accounts. Don't use expensive services to accomplish this.

- Make sure to obtain your own credit history before you divorce. One spouse may be penalized because the other has not paid debts incurred during the marriage. If there have been credit problems in the family in the past, there are ways in which to reestablish credit. Check into them.

- If there is a joint account, as far as the creditor is concerned, each of you is fully responsible, regardless of what the court order says. This means that if your spouse is obligated to pay a joint debt, or a debt that you have incurred, and doesn't do so, the creditor can sue you for payment. Sure, you can bring a court action to enforce the order, but what if your ex-spouse has left the state? And what about the expense involved?

- Look into how the debts created during the marriage will be divided and paid. And remember, if the other party is required to pay for a car in your name and the other party refuses to do so or leaves the state, you are responsible. The court order has nothing to do with the bank. Look into alternatives to avoid these situations.

- When it comes to dividing up debt, you may want to consider: 1) getting security from the spouse who is obligated to pay the debt—such as a savings account or stock—that will be returned when the obligation is paid but that is available if the obligation is not paid; 2) purchasing a small life/disability insurance policy to secure the obligation; and/or 3) getting the obligated spouse to refinance the account so that it's not in your name or so that your car is not security for the debt.

- Remember: The filing of bankruptcy, either during or after the divorce, may affect your credit and disrupt everything you have planned and paid for. Make sure you talk to your lawyer about this very important area of concern.

Pensions, IRAs, and Social Security

Along with your home, the pension and retirement fund that has been built up during the marriage can make up the bulk of the marital estate. In most states, retirement plans are divisible on divorce. But there are many different kinds of retirement plans and many complex rules. Be sure to discuss with your lawyer the type of plan involved in your situation, and consider the following aspect:

- Find out how pensions and IRAs are valued and divided in your state. Remember, each plan is different and you must be sure that an appropriate court order (called a QDRO— Qualified Domestic Relations Order) is issued. Make sure to determine the tax consequences of pension distributions, and whether you will be affected. And look into roll-over possibilities if the pension is to be divided.

- Generally, the sums that make up a pension fund cannot be used immediately without taxes and penalties—unless you are of the age designated by the plan. But if you decide you need the money, find out first what the penalty is, then decide if the penalty is worth taking out the money.

- There are different types of rules for different types of pensions, and there are alternatives available regarding taking a lump sum or a distribution within a month after retirement. You must determine which rules apply in your case, as far as distributions and roll-overs are concerned. These are complex questions that your lawyer should answer for you.

- Research the best place to invest (roll over) these sums safely pending withdrawal, but be careful. Remain conservative and don't take risks.

- Social Security entitlement must be researched and considered before divorce. Generally, if a marriage has lasted for ten years or more, a 62-year-old, non-wage-earning spouse has the right to draw on the wage earner's benefits, even if the wage earner has not begun drawing benefits. A trip to your local Social Security office will provide answers to many of these questions, including the amounts and taxation effects of these payments.

- Military and civil service pensions are handled differently. You may want to check with the local Judge Advocate's office or civil service office for the latest survivor beneficiary rules. Or, call your congressman or senator.

Once You Get It, You Need to Keep It

The breakup of a marriage is like the breakup of a business partnership. The assets and the liabilities are going to be divided. The method by which the property is divided varies from state to state, and may be called community property, equitable distribution, or equitable division. But whatever it is called, whenever you get your share, you must be prepared to "reinvest it wisely" because in many cases, this is all you are going to get. **Ninety percent of those who get a lump sum today will not have it within five years.**

- Since you will be changing your life status and either handling money for the first time or modifying your lifestyle, you need to figure out what is best for you. You will find that there are complex and confusing options out there; there are also many salespeople, each of whom has all of the "right answers." Never be suckered into a high-return deal because high return means high risk…and you can't afford it.

- Consumers lose more than $500 million annually to unscrupulous planners and salespeople, so make sure the person in whom you are about to place your trust—and your money— can deliver to suit your needs. Before you write the check to put your financial future in the hands of a financial planner or anyone else, check out the situation thoroughly.

- If your lifestyle is based not only on alimony and support but also on interest derived from investments, look for the best way to ensure that this interest income continues to be paid while, at the same time, protecting your principal.

- Your plan must be arranged for a particular need without the risks of high fees, commissions, and high-risk financial products. Always ask about commissions and keep track of what is being done with your money.

- Look carefully, because there are all types of investments—and some don't look like investments. For example, you may be approached with insurance products that are really investments. Understand what you're getting before you write that check.

- Get everything in writing before you decide where to put your money. This is also true when it comes to dealing with insurance salesmen, brokers, or financial planners. In fact, more insurance salesmen have securities licenses today than do brokers—and they sell both insurance and investments.

- Mutual funds are securities that are sold by insurance salesmen, financial planners, and brokers alike. But all mutual funds are not safe investments. Before you invest, make sure you find out about the amount of sales commissions, and how much you will be penalized if you decide to remove your money at any point during the first four years.

- Avoid high-risk investments and "churning" of accounts. ("Churning" is a practice whereby trades are made in an account not for the benefit of the holder of the assets, but for the broker to earn commissions.)

- Salespeople may try to sell you annuities, telling you that you need a steady flow of revenue. Check these out and understand annuities before you invest, because if you need the money too soon, you will be penalized substantially if you take it out. And, always check out the financial stability of the company behind the annuity. Many insurance companies today are thinly capitalized, which means that you may lose your investment if the company goes under.

- Understand that you may have more education than your adviser: 6 percent of planners do not have high school diplomas, compared to only 1 percent of clients.

- Being designated a Certified Financial Planner (CFP) or a Chartered Financial Consultant (ChFC) means the planner passed a series of tests given by trade associations—little more. Almost anyone can use the title "Financial Planner," and between 150,000 and 500,000 people do so. Becoming a Registered Investment Advisor (RIA) with the Securities and Exchange Commission means little more than completing a questionnaire and paying a $150 registration fee.

- Many "planners" have less than ten years' experience, so find out how long, and where, they have been in business. Be sure to obtain and check bank references, client references, and references from professionals, such as lawyers and accountants who have used the planner.

- Find out if the planner has ever been sued and if he or she has errors insurance and omissions insurance, just in case there is a problem. Ask where his or her own money is invested, and determine how their investments are doing. If the planner won't answer you or hedges on a response, look elsewhere.

- Avoid those planners who hedge on describing how they are compensated. Some may derive most of their income from commissions on products they suggest to you. Although 85 percent of planners sell financial products, only 47 percent tell the client that this is the source of their (the planner's) income.

- Fee-only planners may be more objective than those charging commissions, but their upfront charges may be more. Be sure to find out how many times per year the fee will be charged, and make sure the charges are "fee only."

- Other planners may charge a combination of fees and commissions. Make sure you get the entire cost up front and in writing—and compare the costs with other options.

- Steer clear of high-risk products, promises of "guaranteed returns," and "risk-free investments." Watch out for those who want a power of attorney and discretion over your assets. *Never* grant this. Stay away from limited partnerships and other assets that are hard to value and cannot be readily sold if you need the cash. There are thousands of financial products out there, so *be careful.*

- If you don't understand it, don't do it. Don't be forced into anything. Don't be intimidated. Get it in writing. Know with whom
you are dealing and the strategy that suits you *before* you make
a deal.

Estate Planning Is Part of Divorce

Of all adults in the United States, 70 percent have never written a
will. You can't afford to be one of those. Consider the following:

- Change your will after divorce or remarriage. And, consider
an interim will immediately upon separation to ensure that the
estate won't pass to an estranged spouse. Make sure to change
the beneficiaries on your life and accident policies, whether
work-related or individually owned. Don't put it off.

- Your estate can be structured to provide for minor children by
the use of trusts, springing powers of attorney, and guardianships. Check into this because it is an important part of your
transition, and if you don't do it now, you probably never will.

- Always spell out guardianship provisions in your will. If you
don't specify how you want your children raised, a court will
do it for you, without you being there to object.

- There are many kinds of trusts available, and insurance policies
can have trusts as beneficiaries. Choose custodians and trustees
carefully, and talk to them before you name them. Consider a
friend or relative in close proximity to avoid changing schools.

- If a disabled child is involved, there are special concerns in
estate planning. Find a lawyer who is an expert in this area
because he/she can save you time, money, and aggravation.
Ask about a discretionary spendthrift trust to supplement
government assistance.

- Look into "living wills" (which take care of such things as taking you off respirators when you can't make the decisions for yourself), and make sure you have a power of attorney in place so that someone can make these and other decisions if you become disabled. This will save time, money, and trouble later.

- Inquire about what happens if you or a loved one are put into a nursing home, because this type of care usually is not covered by traditional health insurance, meaning the assets you fought so hard to acquire could go up in smoke.

- Learn about contracts to make wills, workers compensation coverage beneficiaries, and "key man" coverage beneficiaries.

- Always ask your professional planner about the tax consequences resulting from the way your estate is set up.

The Final Decree May Never Be Final

The decree is signed, and everyone goes in separate directions. Finally, the case is over. Well, not quite.

Both of you will continue to have contact through economic transactions, support payments, and child custody and visitation (if you still have minor children). And, things change after divorce: One or both of you remarries, interjecting new personalities into the situation. One or both of you moves. One needs more money, and the other can't afford the payments. One makes more money and is asked to increase the payments, or the other becomes ill and can't make payments at all. One of you files bankruptcy. And so it goes.

Statistics tell us that one or both of you will want changes made in the agreement or court order to solve an ambiguity in your papers or because something comes up that no one expected. Then what happens? Generally, the whole process starts over again:

Accusations are made. Expenses are inspected. Assets are reap-
praised. A new spouse's income and assets are looked into. You are
thrown back into the judicial system. There are depositions, court
proceedings, lawyers, fees, and expenses all over again. Your lives
are disrupted once again.

Expect and begin to plan now for changes in what you both
thought was a "final settlement." Realize that no lawyer can prepare
or negotiate the perfect agreement that will never be modified,
or will not be subject to two differing interpretations. As long as
people change and circumstances change, it will be necessary to
modify your documents.

Child support payments are always subject to change—either
increased or decreased—if there are significant changes in the
financial circumstances of either parent. Alimony payments may
or may not be modified, depending on how the agreement or court
order is worded. If applicable, custody and visitation are always
open to change if the best interests of the children would be served
by change. Property settlements are generally not subject to change,
but may be dischargeable in bankruptcy.

You can't stop change, so you might want to discuss with your
lawyer alternatives that may help when modification arises, such as:

- Penalty clauses: If one of you brings an action that is determined by the court to be frivolous or results in less than what
  is asked for, the party who causes the litigation will be required
  to pay all expenses and attorneys' fees.

- Incentive clauses: Rather than litigate each time a financial
  change occurs, think about an income disclosure system
  whereby, for example, if a non-working spouse begins working, alimony is reduced by a fixed sum based upon each dollar
  earned—for example, by twenty-five cents. So, if alimony is set

at $500 per month for an unemployed spouse, and that person begins working and earns $1,000 per month, alimony would be reduced by $250 per month.

- Alternatives to litigation: Both of you can agree to take many of your disputes out of the court system. This doesn't mean that you don't need lawyers; it simply means that you can agree on the methods and procedures by which disputes can be resolved privately and in less time.

- A mediation clause: This can provide both of you with a non-adversarial atmosphere where you are in charge of what is happening to you. You and your ex-spouse may be able to construct your own agreement, one you both can live with. If not, since mediation is not binding, you can always choose to go to court.

- An arbitration clause: This can provide a binding way by which to avoid the court system when disputes arise that cannot be resolved through agreements.

In any case, before you agree to anything, discuss the pros and cons with your lawyer.

Don't Forget about Uncle Sam

Divorce means much more than terminating a marriage, agreeing on the amount of child support if you still have minor children, setting a visitation schedule (again, if you still have minor children), and going your own way. Consider the following:

- Divorce means transfers and sales of property; payments of money; changes in economic conditions and positions; estate and retirement planning; wills, gifts, and trusts—and much more. And, any time there is a transfer or a payment, either now or in the future, you must be made aware of and consider income, gift, and estate tax consequences.

- Sometimes, people don't know that a gift has been made and a tax is due until it's too late. Many people don't know that the way property is titled, and who has the control over the property, can make the difference between tax and no tax.

- You don't need to know all of the rules that apply in each of these complex areas, but you do need to make sure that all of your taxation questions are identified and answered before you begin paying or receiving funds, transferring or receiving property, paying debts, or signing wills and trusts.

- Audits of tax returns filed during the marriage that occur after the divorce has been finalized must be addressed in your divorce. These audits generally involve both the husband and the wife, and they can be expensive. Since husbands and wives are generally jointly and individually liable for the entire tax due on a joint return—regardless of who earned the income and provided the information—either can be required to pay past-due taxes and penalties. If you were not the primary wage earner but signed the returns, try to protect yourself by including in your divorce settlement an agreement that if there is an audit, you will be indemnified from all expense and tax liability by your spouse. Although not binding on the IRS, this can give you some degree of protection on a reimbursement basis.

- If you borrow substantial funds from relatives and don't make repayment, the loan may be considered to be a gift to you, and your relatives might be required to pay a gift tax. If you don't pay interest or the interest is forgiven, your relatives may be taxed as though they had received from you what the interest should have been, and then gave it back to you as a gift.

- Legal expenses for a divorce are not deductible from income for tax purposes, but if you pay fees for tax advice, you can deduct that portion of fees. Ask your lawyer to maintain separate records concerning the tax aspects of your case. If you hire a separate tax lawyer or CPA to advise you on the tax consequences, and you pay the fees, you should be able to qualify for a deduction.

What Is It All Going to Cost?

Now that you've gotten all of your ducks in a row, you should talk to your lawyer about cost:

- You will probably be asked to pay a retainer and sign a contract before a lawyer will handle your case. This is normal; however, you should discuss and understand these issues before you enter into this relationship. In your first meeting with your lawyer, you should discuss cost.

- Understand how the lawyer's fees are computed, the best estimate of the range of fees, and the probable expenses to handle your case. Have a clear, written understanding about how the fees are payable, and when. This will save you from later misunderstandings.

- Find out if a legal secretary, legal assistant, or paralegal will be assigned to your case for preparation purposes. If so, don't feel that you are getting "second class" treatment. These people are well-trained professionals, and their services are billed at lower rates than those of your lawyer.

- Generally, other experts are necessary to help prepare your case. CPAs, business analysts, appraisers, and others often are needed to help your lawyer determine valuation, taxation, and other issues. Determine the range of these fees, how the fees are charged, and how they are payable. You don't need any surprises.

Take Stock of the Entire Situation

Now that you have asked the important economic questions and received some of the answers, you must ask yourself and your lawyer several additional questions before you make final decisions:

- Are all of my goals worth the cost?

- Is the chance of success sufficient to go after each goal, or should some goals be given a lesser priority, or be negotiated, or be forgotten?

- Is the time, stress, and cost of a full-blown war worth it? Or, is there a way to fairly resolve the most important issues more quickly?

- Consider "cost" in terms of both time and money. If I offer to pay you $5 today or promise to pay you $10 two years from today, which would you take? First, ask yourself several questions:

  - Where will the person who made the promise be next year when it's time to fulfill the promise?

  - Will the person who made the promise be able to keep the promise next year?

  - How much will it cost to collect on that promise?

  - What security is being put up to ensure that the promise will be enforced?

  - If I take the $5 today, what has it cost me to get it, what could I earn with it by next year if I had it today, and what could that $5 be worth by next year? Obviously, if it costs $5 to get the $10 promise and the promise is not kept, you are out $5. Deciding whether to accept an offer or not is based on much the same rationale.

QUESTION: *Our 32-year-old daughter has confided to us that she wants a divorce after eight years of marriage. She and her husband have no children. Our daughter is a teacher, and she doesn't make a lot of money; her husband is a salesman and doesn't make a huge salary, either. Her mother and I want to make sure that she is well-represented and gets a fair settlement. She is our only child. What kinds of things does she need to know?*

ANSWER: You should help your daughter remember that panic and emotions have no place in the decision-making process; that she should keep her goals in perspective and not allow her lawyer to make her decisions for her; that she should negotiate as many issues as possible *after* she has become informed; that she and her husband should each have their own lawyer; that fighting just to fight is a bad business decision.

We would also suggest that she buy a notebook and put all of her questions and concerns in writing before she meets with her lawyer. She should prepare a budget and review all expenses so that she has an idea of how much it will take her to live on her own. She should also list all assets, including cost and estimated current values; she should also itemize debts. If she can, your daughter should photocopy and photograph every financial record and piece of property, and then keep the copies in a safe place.

Finally, if you are able, it would be a good idea to help your daughter pay for a good divorce lawyer. More often than not, a good outcome for her will depend on the competence of her attorney.

12

Second, Third, and Beyond Marriages

Who says we learn by experience? One of two first marriages ends in divorce, but six of ten second marriages end the same way. And, most of us still don't know our rights, even if we've been divorced before. We're sadder, but not much wiser. On top of this, second-marriage mortality rates are higher than those of first marriages because the issues are much more complex.

For example, people marry later today, and they have more assets. More married women work outside the home after children are born, and an increasing number are beginning to manage their personal assets. Couples are bringing more children from first marriages into second marriages. (There are more than 35 million step-parent households in the United States, and by the time children reach seventh grade, half no longer live with both natural parents.)

All of this makes marriage and re-marriage more complex, which is why couples need to plan carefully and protect themselves. Here are ways to do this:

- A reasonable couple, not the courts, can decide through planning how their property is to be divided. This brings predictability to the relationship. Those who have wealth usually plan well before marriage—but all of us should know and protect our rights, because if average-income people lose half of what they have, it will hurt them far more than wealthier people.

- Never get married the second time without a better understanding of your legal rights and duties than you had the first time. Don't marry the second time without planning for the contingencies. You need information to help make intelligent choices.

- Many marry the second time without considering that by court order, the first obligation is to their children by the prior marriage, and to Spouse #1, who receives support.

- Spouse #1 may look upon the second marriage with jealousy and envy. The return from the honeymoon is often met by legal papers asking for more support. And Spouse #2's income is often considered in judging the ability to pay increased support.

- Women may marry the second time without any idea that the new husband owes support arrearages to Spouse #1, or is in substantial debt. And so, soon after the marriage, Wife #2's assets and income are being used to keep him out of jail or to pay his debts.

- Men may marry the second time only to find themselves supporting the stepchildren because Husband #1 has left the state or won't pay support. Husband #2 finds himself assuming the new wife's debts, which he didn't anticipate or want.

- No one entering a second marriage should assume that the amount of support being paid to Family #1 will always remain the same. When a non-custodial father, who is paying support to Family #1, takes on a second family, he is often considered to be voluntarily assuming new obligations. And the new wife's income may be considered in a suit to increase support payments to Family #1.

- "Prenuptial Agreement" is not a bad term. It is simply a written contract entered into before the marriage that changes how the law would normally deal with property, income, and other responsibilities *if* the marriage ends by death or divorce. A prenuptial agreement is really a combination of estate, retirement, and life management plans all rolled into one.

- Appropriately prepared, prenuptial agreements can guarantee predictability if the marriage ends by death or divorce. Assets can be kept separate or shared as agreed upon. Children by prior marriages can be protected. Financial security for a spouse and children can be accomplished. Those who marry for companionship, not financial security, can protect their estates for their families.

- To be valid, everyone must be treated fairly. Both spouses-to-be must give and receive full financial disclosure before signing the prenuptial agreement. Both must have their own lawyer, and the agreement must be voluntary. A prenuptial agreement is not for a person who may want to hide things, because such an agreement will surely be set aside by the courts if the couple eventually separates and wants to divorce .

- Taxes are a big consideration. Each taxpayer who signs a joint return is responsible for all taxes and information on the tax return. For example, if you marry on December 31 and earned no income that year but signed the return, and there is an audit, you are responsible for all information and liable for all taxes due. You should, at a minimum, get a "hold harmless" agreement before you sign those returns.

- Financial stability is another big consideration. Before you marry, you both need to be able to plan. If your intended is unwilling to make disclosures, this might indicate a secret. And being secretive before the marriage tells you something about how the marriage is likely to turn out.

- Estate planning directs what is to be done after death and, while living, through trusts, gifts, and insurance. If you enter a pre-nuptial agreement, you can handle your estate plans at the same time. And remember, you need wills to make sure your agreement is implemented.

Not everyone who falls in love, of course, will decide to marry again—or even to marry for the first time. Our next chapter discusses how living together (cohabitation), or entering into a domestic partnership, will affect your planning.

Question: *I am a 71-year-old widow, and I plan to marry a man eight years younger than I. While I have been told by my lawyer and family to get a premarital agreement, I have not brought it up because I am afraid talking about this topic will ruin our relationship. Yet, I want to make sure my three children by my deceased husband receive their fair share. My biggest assets are a home, some cash, and several IRAs that I received when my husband died. I also receive a tax-free amount each month from a structured settlement because my husband was killed in an automobile accident. This money will last for fifteen more years at a minimum. Are there ways for me to transfer my assets and prepare a will that protects my children without a premarital agreement—yet treats my husband fairly?*

Answer: Although premarital agreements are certainly not for everyone, they are sometimes necessary to not only spell out what happens in the event of a separation or divorce, but also if you predecease your new spouse. We don't suggest that you gift your assets to your children because you will lose control and create potential tax problems.

That said, there are a number of ways in which you can position your property to protect it, but the planning process will depend on the law of the state where you live and is much too complex to be covered here. For example, if you transfer your assets into a revocable trust to try to keep your spouse from getting part of your estate, the courts in some states will look through the trust as if it did not exist because you still control the assets. On the other hand, if you transfer assets into an irrevocable trust, you may be able to keep these assets away from your spouse when you die, but you give up control over your properties during your life and could trigger taxation problems you may not expect.

Again, depending on where you live and whether or not you will have a taxable estate, a good middle ground might be to consider a will that includes "qualified terminable interest property" (QTIP) trust provisions. In this way, you can not only give your spouse an income interest in certain property during his life and direct where the balance goes at his death, but also pass the majority of your assets to your children at your death. You will not only retain control over the final disposition of your assets, but also make sure your children are protected—even if your second spouse remarries after your death. You could also make your children the beneficiaries of your IRAs.

However, if talking about financial issues before you marry will sour your relationship, and if you are looking for ways to preserve your assets that do not need to be discussed with your future spouse, we suggest that you think twice about becoming permanently attached to this gentleman because this does not appear to be a good way to start a new marriage.

13

Cohabitation and Domestic Partnerships

We have all heard the terms "domestic partners" and "unmarried cohabitants." No matter the moniker, when two people live together without the benefit of matrimony—whether they are of the same or opposite sex—the planning is the same. And, because each situation is different, because you have many issues to consider, and because no single document can solve your problems, you must take a coordinated approach to the planning process.

Moreover, because the issues surrounding unmarried couples are complex, you and your partner should not attempt to make final decisions until you seek competent legal help. Since matrimonial, estate planning, and elder law attorneys are professionals who deal with relationships every day and are adept at planning and tax-related matters that may affect you and your partner, they may best fill the bill. If you are a gay couple, you should seek information from local lesbian and gay business guilds or community organizations that can recommend a lawyer who is knowledgeable and qualified to advise you.

No matter what else you do, it is wise to sign a cohabitation agreement before you finalize your plans. A cohabitation agreement is a written contract that can regulate your future relationship and allow you to retain control of your lives.

Before you enter into such an agreement, however, you and your partner should disclose and evaluate all of the potential trouble spots and discuss and get answers to the economic and other questions that concern both of you.

If You've Been Married Before

Living together can be especially tricky for individuals after one or both partners has had a traditional marriage. These folks may be faced with obligations to an ex-spouse and children, not to mention anger, jealousy, and other complex issues that will be carried into the new relationship. This can make a cohabitation relationship more stressful and more difficult than a traditional marriage.

If you have been married before and you decide to cohabitate, you'll find that the major trouble spots will concern issues relating to children and finances. Even if the children are already grown, there can still be problems. Consider the following story:

> Geoff, a retired schoolteacher, and his wife divorced after 35 years of marriage. Their two children were grown. Later, Geoff met Stella, a widow who had three grown children. The couple decided to move in together. Stella sold her home and moved into Geoff's house, and they shared expenses. Both Geoff's and Stella's children objected to the arrangement, however. None of the children would celebrate holidays with the couple. After a year, Stella moved out.

If children from a previous marriage are still minors when you and your partner decide to live together, you should know that custody disputes can arise at any time and for a variety of reasons—some of which relate to the legitimate best interests of a child, others which relate to financial issues, control, and so on.

If a custody dispute arises, in addition to significant expense for lawyers and experts, not to mention discovery and court costs, you can expect the polarization of families and friends, grandparents asserting their rights, continuing emotional crisis for the children, personal lives becoming public information, and years of turmoil.

Also, there are the potential financial land mines. After entering a live-in relationship, what if you learn that, despite the new Lexus your partner is driving, he or she has a poor financial history, owes past-due child support, has judgments against him/her that prevent the property ownership, or has recently gone through bankruptcy. Even worse, you find out that your income may be considered in a lawsuit to increase the child support or alimony payments of your live-in partner. And, the cost of hiring lawyers and going to court can be out-of-sight.

If cohabiting couples don't check out the finances of their partners, and don't know that child support or alimony is past due, or money is owed for a business deal, or there has been a bankruptcy, the new relationship can be compromised early. And, although there is no legal obligation to help, faced with a Catch-22 situation of either trying to make the relationship work or losing a partner, some will opt to write a check. Homes and retirements have been lost to bail out a new partner, who later bails out of the relationship.

Bottom line: You and your partner should both give and receive full financial disclosure so there will be no surprises later. Don't be afraid to ask questions and to review (or have some knowledge-able person review for you) the last five years of your partner's tax returns. And, let him or her review yours.

In addition, why not exchange credit reports? Review divorce decrees and support orders? Look at employee benefits and insurance policies? Discuss and agree upon who is going to pay for what? If either of you has children, you should consider estate planning to protect them. Get new wills and sign durable powers of attorney for financial purposes.

Why Estate Planning Is Essential

Consider the following true story:

> *After moving in together, purchasing a home, and pledging their love—without a marriage ceremony and against the wishes of their adult children—Tom and Karen had everything going for them. Everything, that is, until Tom was involved in a serious automobile accident that resulted in severe and permanent physical and neurological injuries that not only affected his ability to communicate, but also rendered him unable to care for himself.*

Had Tom and Karen been officially married, Karen would have been by Tom's side in the hospital, would have helped him through his rehabilitation, and would have been legally responsible for Tom's care and financial affairs after discharge without so much as a question.

Because they were not married and the law did not recognize their relationship, however, Tom's children, not Karen, were first in line to become Tom's legal guardians. As his legal guardians, Tom's children became legally responsible for their father, and they controlled not only his financial affairs and medical treatment decisions, but also who would, and would not, visit him in the hospital. They also controlled where he would live.

While he was still able to make decisions, Tom could have chosen what medical treatment he wanted (or didn't want) and he could have appointed Karen to make medical and financial decisions for him if he were unable to do so. Since he did not, it was almost impossible for Karen to prove to the court what Tom's wishes really were. Unwittingly, Tom forfeited control of his life to the state and its courts, placing quite an unintended burden on his partner.

Today, more than ever, unmarried cohabitants must be attuned to the issues, become informed, and attempt to avoid what could otherwise be disastrous consequences.

Coordinated planning and use of written documents is especially important for unmarried couples. Because they are not considered to be "family," without a health care power of attorney, for example, one partner will have no say in health-care decisions of the other, and may not even be able to visit the other partner in the hospital. Because relationships between unmarried couples are not recognized by state inheritance laws, wills are essential to assure that planned distributions of assets are not frustrated. And, because an unmarried partner is not considered to be a relative, without a durable power of attorney a court-appointed conservator may be appointed to handle the financial decisions of the other partner if he or she becomes incompetent.

You and your partner have the opportunity to prepare for your future. If you have already done so, it does not hurt to review your plan every year or two to make sure you have left nothing out, or that nothing has changed.

Finally, because of the importance of the ancillary issues involving unmarried couples and because there are some technicalities to be avoided, a lawyer should help you and your partner prepare your will and your other documents. It is most unfortunate to see a home-made will or health care power of attorney challenged and set aside by the courts because someone failed to dot the "i's" or cross the "t's," especially for unmarried couples who have no other options available.

The cost of the planning process and of these important documents, when compared to the big picture, is not great, but the protection and the peace of mind these documents afford is priceless.

Essential Planning Tools

Note: We are going to repeat some definitions from earlier chapters because they will be used in a special context here: for unmarried cohabitants.

Power of Attorney

A power of attorney is a written document by which you give any person over the age of 18—called an attorney-in-fact, a proxy, or an agent—the legal authority to act for you under certain circumstances. All states authorize these documents, and some allow an agent to make both property and medical decisions.

Through a power of attorney, you decide and control how much power to give your agent and under what conditions the power may be exercised. For example, you may give your partner the authority to deal only with one piece of your property or with all of your property. You may give your partner the power to act immediately or only if you become incapacitated.

There are two basic kinds of powers of attorney:

1) A **regular power of attorney**, whereby your agent's power begins when you sign and ends when you die or become incapacitated. This means that if you become incapacitated, your partner could be in the same position that Karen found herself in, contesting claims by your blood relatives who are trying to get the court to appoint a guardian or conservator to handle your financial affairs. *This is not the type of document you want.*

2) A **durable power of attorney**, through which your agent's power begins when you sign, remains in effect even if you become incapacitated, and terminates on your death (when your will takes over). You'll want to consider a durable power of attorney because if you become incapacitated, your partner will be able to take over the financial aspects of your

partnership immediately and, unless there is a court challenge by family members, your partner should be spared the expense of legal proceedings.

If you don't want your partner's authority to become effective until you become incapacitated, you may want to consider a type of durable power of attorney called a "springing durable power of attorney." Here, the authority "springs" into effect when you become unable to act for yourself.

Remember: You can change or cancel a power of attorney at any time after you sign it, so long as you still have mental capacity and follow with the law of the state of residence.

A Will

Through a will, you control what happens to your property at your death. Since a will does not become effective until you die, you may change or cancel it at any time after you sign it, so long as you still have mental capacity and follow the law of the state where you live. Without a will, you forfeit your right to direct where your property goes when you die. This means that since you and your partner are not related by blood or marriage, he or she will receive nothing. Without a will, unintended results will occur.

A will not only distributes your property in the way you desire after death, but also names the person whom you want to administer your estate. You can provide burial instructions, appoint trustees, and, depending on how your will is prepared, even be able to save your estate from taxes. You and your partner may want to consider the use of reciprocal wills with "no contest" provisions to attempt to discourage later attacks. To do this, property or money is left to one or more blood relatives who are most likely to later attack the will. Should there be an attack, then the "devise or bequest" to those relatives is cancelled.

Living Trusts

For unmarried couples, "living trusts" can be part of a coordinated plan that may not only reduce the potential of challenges by families but also provide an easier transition should death or disability of a partner occur.

A living trust is a revocable trust, meaning that you can change or terminate it at any time while you are competent. If properly prepared and implemented, a living trust can allow you to carry out your wishes in both life and death, leave you in charge of your wealth until you die, and avoid probate. Before you choose to use a revocable living trust, however, you should make sure you understand the long-term effects and what will, and won't, work effectively for you and your partner.

Since there are no tax benefits involved if you choose to use a living trust, your estate will still include whatever assets may be transferred into the trust.

Irrevocable Trusts and Limited Partnerships

If your assets include a business owned and operated by you and your partner, you should both be concerned about the issue of business continuation and succession—that is, how the business will continue after your death and how to make sure your partner receives it without claim by others. Unfortunately, without planning, should anything happen to you, your partner may find himself or herself with unwanted "new partners," and the business may be sold to try to raise cash to pay unexpected estate taxes or as part of a dissolution. By use of irrevocable trusts and limited partnerships, many of these questions may be satisfactorily resolved in flexible ways.

Health Care Planning

Today, with the cost of health care and long-term nursing home care reaching astronomical proportions, you and your partner must also plan for health care and long-term care in addition to the traditional planning we have just described. Without filling in these important pieces of the puzzle, the rest of your planning strategy may be wasted.

Advance health care directives are documents you can use to express your wishes about your future medical treatment. These documents do not take effect until you become incapacitated and are unable to make decisions. Until then, you can change or revoke them. Since the law of each state is different, we will talk about the basics of the most common advance directives that can be useful to you and your live-in partner.

The Living Will and Health Care Power of Attorney

The living will (see Chapter 6) is the best-known type of advance directive. There is also the durable health care power of attorney (see Chapter 6), also called a health care power of attorney.

Some states have specific laws that authorize the appointment of a health-care agent, while others rely on court decisions. Where authorized by state law, the durable health care power of attorney can help you and your partner overcome many of the limitations created by living wills. Through a durable health care power of attorney, you can direct that *everything* possible be done to preserve your life, that *nothing* be done, or that some procedures be done and others not be done. You can make the document flexible enough to deal with unforeseen developments by giving your agent the authority to act as he or she sees fit, or you can specifically limit your agent's authority to act.

Your most important decision before signing a health care power of attorney is choosing the person you want to act as your agent, and discussing your intentions with him or her. Your health-care agent need not be your partner. After you sign the document, you should give your agent a list of your health-care desires, including your feelings about life support and extraordinary life-prolonging medical procedures. Then if your agent is called on later to make decisions, he or she will be able to act effectively on your behalf and, it is hoped, eliminate partner-family disputes that can occur during these trying times.

Where to Put These Documents

After you sign your documents, you should put your will and power of attorney in a safe place, such as your safe deposit box, or leave it with your lawyer. It is a good idea for you and your partner to give each other signed copies to keep. Don't forget to tell the person whom you have chosen to become the personal representative of your estate where the document is kept. In some states, a power of attorney must be filed with the records of the clerk of court. Be sure to ask your lawyer about the rules in your state.

Your health-care documents should also be placed in a safe place, but not a safety deposit box. We suggest that you give copies of these documents to your partner, your doctor, and close friends, because these documents will do you no good if the people who will be around you in the hospital don't know they exist. We also suggest that you talk with your doctor to make sure he or she understands your desires, and be sure to use the opportunity to introduce your partner to this important health-care provider.

Since most legal contests are based on undue influence or fraud, or a combination of the two, you might consider trying to head off a potential contest by sending copies of your health care power of attorney, and even your will and power of attorney, to your blood relatives. With these documents in hand and written knowledge of your relationship with your partner before the fact, you may be able to head off, or take much of the sizzle out of, a later claim. To have proof later that you were not the victim of fraud and undue influence, consider videotaping the signing in the lawyer's office.

Other Issues: Co-Ownership Agreements

John, 67, and Kim, 62, his live-in partner of six years, are both divorced. Neither want to get married, but they do want to purchase a home together. John is retired, but Kim still works and is willing to contribute to the purchase price and make monthly payments. They went to a lawyer who told them that all they needed to do was to put the home in their joint names with a provision that the survivor would receive the share of the first of them to die. But they want to leave their shares to their children at the time of the second death.

Buying the house may be relatively easy, but disentangling yourselves from the arrangement should your relationship terminate—or when one of you dies—can be most difficult and expensive because then you won't have the remedies that are available to married couples. Despite the way the law may look at your relationship, when you purchase a residence together, you become "married" financially. That's why it's best to plan ahead, design your remedies, and to try to avoid the many potential pitfalls through a "co-ownership agreement" at the time you purchase property.

Without a co-ownership agreement that clearly defines your intentions and mechanisms to resolve any disputes, you will be forced to depend upon expensive, yet inadequate, legal remedies that will probably not reflect your intentions. And since there are not automatic inheritance laws, you must plan for what will become of the property when one of you dies. This means that a lawyer (probably one for each party) should be consulted to prepare a cohabitation agreement. These documents are enforceable in the court system if properly prepared after financial disclosure.

In addition, contracts to make wills can be prepared to "set in stone" postmortem intentions. But remember: If the relationship goes south, the documents you have prepared must be revoked, based on terms set forth in the agreements.

Still, not being governed by specialized laws and procedures can be an opportunity: You and your partner can plan now to anticipate future problems and create ways to avoid disputes.

Before you and your partner take title to a residence, you should understand that the way in which the property is titled can carry with it a number of unforeseen consequences. It is unwise to have title placed in the name of only one partner, even for "tax purposes," because if that person sells the home and keeps the money, or dies and leaves it to antagonistic relatives, you could be in court for a long time and lose your investment. Depending on where you live, therefore, the two types of ownership you and your partner should consider are joint tenancy and tenancy in common.

Because state laws involving marriage are based on the unity of a couple's life and assets, married couples often take title as joint tenants. In this way, neither owner can change the title without the consent of the other. And no matter what the deceased spouse's will may say to the contrary, the surviving spouse-owner will inherit the interest of the deceased spouse, subject to outstanding mortgages and liens.

Joint tenancy can also be used by some cohabiting partners. (It cannot be used if the owners do not own the property in equal shares.) While joint tenancy has its benefits for unmarried cohabitants—such as no probate upon the death of one partner—there are also drawbacks, legal ramifications, and difficulties should the relationship terminate by mutual consent.

In contrast, since the economic relationship of unmarried partners is not governed by state law and reflects "separateness" rather than a combination of resources and obligations, tenancy in common is probably a better choice in most instances. As tenants in common, you and your partner have the right to name by will who inherits your share of the property. This means that if you die, your share of the property passes to whomever you choose in your will, subject to outstanding liens. And, if you don't have a will, your share will pass to those members of your family who are automatically selected by state law. In other words, your co-owner partner has no self-operating right to your share of the property, not even a right of purchase, unless this right is provided for in your co-ownership agreement.

For these and other reasons, should you decide to choose tenancy in common, you and your partner should make sure to deal with your estate plans because, if either of you dies without a will, the survivor may become a co-owner with members of the deceased partner's immediate family, who may or may not have approved of your relationship in the first place. You may also want to discuss with your lawyer the benefits of using a revocable living trust before you make any final decisions.

Apportioning Ownership and Dividing Proceeds

The way in which your property is titled can also be a method by which you and your partner apportion ownership and divide proceeds on sale. For example, if your comparative initial contributions and continued payments justify it, title ownership could be allocated 60 percent to you and 40 percent to your partner. But in many instances, this could lead to an unfair division of the sales proceeds—for example, if you and your partner make unequal portions of the down payment but pay equally toward mortgage payments, taxes, and maintenance, or if there is significant appreciation in value. Even if you and your partner have made unequal contributions, dividing the proceeds can also lead to disputes. What this all means is that your plans and intentions should be clearly dealt with in a co-ownership agreement that addresses your intentions and the potential contingencies before the fact, not later, when there are no options.

If you contribute all or the larger share of the down payment, here are two of the ways for you to be repaid when the property is sold:

- You and your partner could agree that at the time of sale, each of you would first be reimbursed your contributions, and the excess would then be divided equally. So, let's assume that John and Kim buy a home for $100,000. John puts down $25,000, Kim contributes $10,000, and they jointly take out a $65,000 mortgage. If they later sell the home for $150,000.00, under this scenario, after paying off the mortgage balance, John would receive his $25,000.00 down payment plus half of the remaining equity, and Kim would receive her $10,000.00 down payment plus half of the remaining equity. The problem here is that by simply refunding the initial contributions, Kim will receive the same gain on a $10,000 investment as John will on a $25,000 investment, and John will lose the appreciation attributable to his greater contributions.

- Another alternative would be for John and Kim to agree to divide the sales proceeds in the same percentages as their initial contributions. Since John's contribution to the down payment under this example was 71 percent, John would receive 71 percent of total equity and Kim would receive 29 percent of total equity. But there is also a problem here: If John and Kim equally paid the mortgage, taxes, insurance, and maintenance payments, Kim would come up short.

Using either method brings with it both pluses and minuses. That's why some people develop their own formulas to try to factor in the actual contributions and appreciation. But when you begin to consider improvements to the property, the calculations become even more difficult. For example, what if, in addition to making the down payments, John and Kim each paid $7,500 toward property improvements? In this case, what part of the gain results from the down payments and what part from the improvements?

There are still other considerations: What if you and your partner agree to contribute equally to all payments and repairs, but one of you does not comply with the agreement? Are there circumstances under which you and your partner would want initial unequal ownership to ripen into equal ownership? How will you handle it if a third person, such as one of your parents, helps by putting up money for the down payment but does not live there? And if the property is sold for a loss, will you and your partner share losses in the same way you share profits?

Paying the Mortgage, Insurance, Taxes, Repairs and Utilities

Some mortgage payments consist of principal and interest, while others also include taxes and insurance. Either way, a co-ownership agreement should provide that you and your partner will each pay half (or whatever percentage you agree upon) of the complete payment each month by the due date. If there is no escrow for taxes or insurance, you and your partner should open a joint account, requiring both signatures, into which each of you should deposit each month agreed shares of the taxes and insurance. This is so that when due, the funds will be there to pay these obligations.

But the basic assumption that you and your partner will pay your share of the mortgage payments each month, not to mention taxes, insurance, utilities, and repairs when due, may be ignored if a dispute results in one of you moving out and needing to pay rent or mortgage payments somewhere else. Under these circumstances, it may be tempting for the vacating partner to ignore his or her obligations, thereby leaving the remaining partner to carry the entire burden in order to continue living in the property.

For these reasons, the co-ownership agreement should contain very specific provisions that will deter the vacating party from ignoring these responsibilities. Penalty provisions, such as meaningful late fees and interest on payments not made on time, should constitute a lien on the vacating party's interest. And if the required payments are not made for, say, six months, consider including a provision by which the vacating partner's interest in the property would be forfeited, thereby allowing the remaining partner to rent or sell the property and keep all of the equity.

Who Pays to Maintain the Residence?

An agreement between you and your partner to pay the necessary maintenance expenses in agreed shares could be more difficult to enforce than you might think. How you and your partner define "necessary" is the key. Repairs to the air conditioner, furnace, water heater, and roof, for example, are clearly necessary, while planting grass and bushes, wallpapering, painting, and putting down new carpet are more voluntary than required.

In order to avoid future disputes, you should not only clearly define what will be done and when, but also who can authorize the work, how the bills will be paid, and in what percentages.

Renting the Residence

What if, in our example, John moves out and Kim can't afford to continue to live there without financial assistance? It might be necessary for the property to be leased in order to defray the monthly mortgage payments and other expenses, or for Kim to bring in a boarder to share expenses. Without a prior written agreement between John and Kim, this remedy will be difficult, if not impossible. That's why your co-ownership agreement should contain rental provisions, including approval of tenants, accountings, and related matters. If the vacating partner is not making payments as called for, the remaining partner should be allowed to make all rental decisions, to collect all rent, and to sign leases and other legal documents.

Options to Purchase and Sell, and Related Issues, During Life

Since the property you and your partner purchase will some day be sold for one reason or another, your co-ownership agreement should contemplate that event and its many nuances. If you and your partner both decide to sell the property at the same time, there should be no problem since both of you will have the same goal: to obtain the best price for the property.

But if only one of you wants to sell, the problems begin: On one hand, the partner who wants to sell his or her interest should not be precluded from disposing of that interest and receiving his or her equity in the property. On the other hand, the partner who wants to continue owning the property should be able to do this, and not be forced to sell off his or her interest. That's why it is best to deal with this issue at the time of purchase in a written agreement when neither partner will be able to predict which one will want to sell in the future.

Again, going back to our example, let's see a couple of ways in which John and Kim can set the purchase price:

- John and Kim could establish a price at the date of purchase and agree to annual increases (or decreases) in value. Since most owners are inexperienced in valuation matters, this is probably not a good idea.

- John and Kim could agree to be bound by the opinion of an independent appraiser who is acceptable to both and whose fees will be paid by them in equal shares. If they can't agree on an appraiser, they might agree that a disinterested person, say, their mortgage lender or banker, will choose the appraiser by whose opinion they both will be bound.

Once the purchase price has been set, the next step is to decide what the buying partner will pay to the selling partner for his or her equity interest. Assuming that the seller owns 50 percent of the property and is up-to-date on all required payments, the following might help establish the amount the seller should receive for his or her equity:

- First, add to half (½) the established sales price the following amounts: half (½) of the escrow balance on deposit with the lender, half (½) of the prorated, prepaid insurance premium, and half (½) of the balance in any common real estate account that has been established by you and your partner.

- Then deduct the following: half (½) of the outstanding mortgage principal balance, half (½) of outstanding taxes prorated to date of sale, half of outstanding utilities and maintenance expenses, and half (½) of interest to be paid with the next mortgage payment prorated from the date of sale to the due date of that payment.

If the selling partner has not paid all agreed obligations, or has made the payments late and penalties and interest have accrued under the co-ownership agreement, then these charges should also be subtracted from the selling partner's share. And, if judgments or other liens have been filed against the seller, these amounts should likewise be deducted and paid to the creditors who otherwise will continue to have a lien against the property after the sale.

After the price has been established, since it will take time to secure the funds required to conclude the buyout, the purchaser should have at least sixty—and probably ninety—days to exercise the purchase option.

Last, but certainly not least, the purchasing partner should be required to either 1) arrange to have the selling partner released from the mortgage or 2) obtain alternative financing by which the original mortgage will be satisfied. It should not be acceptable for the selling partner to have continuing liability on a mortgage after the sale of the residence, especially since most lenders will consider this liability when assessing the selling partner's creditworthiness for obtaining a future loan.

However, getting the mortgage company to release the selling partner from the note and mortgage may be very difficult, if not impossible. Going back to our example, John and Kim used their combined credit to qualify for the mortgage and their combined incomes to make the payments. With John leaving, there will be a drastic drop in available income, to the extent that Kim will probably not be able to qualify for a loan at the time of the buyout if she applies alone—unless the property is a duplex or other multi-family dwelling and rent from other unit(s) may be enough to offset the loss of the John's income.

If Kim can't handle the financial burden of the buyout alone, John might agree to a contract of sale or a second mortgage that will be satisfied with monthly payments. But this, too, is dangerous for a number of reasons: Kim might stop making payments, declare bankruptcy, or allow the property to depreciate. If this method of buyout is being considered, it is a good idea to consider requiring Kim to get the personal guarantee of a financially stable third party to protect John.

Options to Purchase at Death

If one of the partners dies, the survivor should have the option to buy the interest of the deceased from his or her estate on the same terms we have discussed. Because the purchase might be made from an estate (depending on whether or not there are valid wills), the surviving partner may need more time to complete the purchase. If the surviving partner does not exercise the option to purchase, it is a pretty good bet that the property will be sold because the estate and heirs will probably not be interested in assuming this obligation.

Credit Problems

After her divorce, Ann had to pinch her pennies. She had a few revolving charge accounts but never did want credit cards—until she met Ted, who later moved into Ann's apartment. They agreed that since both of them were working, they would split the rent and all other bills equally. Every month, Ted's check was there on time and things were going well. Then, after they had been together for six months, Ted suggested that they open a joint credit card account or two, just in case they needed it. Ann reluctantly filled in and signed the applications Ted brought home. Ann never saw a statement when she picked up the mail and assumed that the cards were not being used. But when Ted moved out nearly nine *months later and moved to another state, Ann found out for the first time that Ted had had the monthly account information sent to his work address and had run up nearly $15,000 in debt. Ann was ultimately responsible for this debt since Ted filed for bankruptcy shortly after leaving.*

How many times have you been asked to sign this or sign that, and you've done it, no questions asked? Many people go through relationships trusting their partners and not realizing the significance of what they have signed until the relationship comes to an end. Then, for the first time, they find out that they are obligated on joint credit cards, retail accounts, or bank loans.

It's important to remember that even though you might not have incurred the debt personally, if you signed to be jointly responsible on the account or bank note, you are just as responsible as your partner. Worse yet, if the obligation is not paid, the creditor has the choice of going after you, your partner, or both of you.

That's why it is essential that full financial disclosures be received and given before you make a commitment to long-range cohabitation. And remember: Even if you and your partner have an agreement that provides who is to pay what obligation and by when, if he or she doesn't do this and skips out, the creditor can still come after you to collect. This is because your agreement with your partner has no effect upon the credit contract with the creditor.

That's why it is very important to find out from each creditor if your signature is on the note, credit application, or debt instrument that was signed by the person or persons responsible for the account. If there is ever a question, you should require the creditor to provide the signature card or other documents and make sure it's your signature. If it's not, and your name was signed by someone else without your authorization, then you may not be responsible.

If you did sign an account—say, at the hardware store—and your partner ran up the bills, make sure to report your situation to the creditor in writing so that this may be taken into consideration if you apply for an individual account. If you are denied credit when you apply for an individual account from anyone, you have the right, by law, to know exactly why your application was turned down.

On a regular basis, you should check your credit report to see if there are any inaccuracies. If there are, give the creditor additional information to show that you are a good credit risk. If this doesn't work, find out which credit service is being used and apply to each individually for correction of your record. This will take time, but detailing that your former partner was responsible should help your record.

Under the Fair Credit Reporting Act, you can learn about your credit rating simply by asking a local credit bureau for a copy of your credit history. You can find a local credit reporting company in the Yellow Pages, and your cost is comparatively minimal. So don't be taken in by advertisements that tout these types of services for a fee. And don't purchase services that, for $100 or $250, claim they will straighten out your credit. Most of these services are scams.

You also need to know that, in most instances, negative information that might appear on a credit record, such as bankruptcy, will generally be removed seven years after it first appears. If you disagree with any information in your report, notify the credit bureau immediately in writing. The bureau must investigate your complaint with the source of the information you dispute.

Another word to the wise: What if you have signed as being obligated on an automobile loan and, as part of your settlement with your partner, he or she is to take the car and agrees to pay off the debt? Make sure he or she refinances the car *before* you transfer title so the debt is in your partner's name, not yours. The same is true of furniture and other installment loans. Remember: Trusting someone with whom you no longer have a relationship to pay your debt is dangerous.

What if you and your partner, as part of your planning, have given each other durable powers of attorney so each of you could make financial decisions for the other? If you don't cancel these documents immediately, there is the potential for abuse.

Dispute Resolution

There are alternative ways to resolve disputes that may arise between you and your partner.

Litigation—going to court with lawyers—is the method of dispute resolution most familiar. If you've ever watched "The People's Court" on television, you may have seen people and their witnesses appear before a judge. After they give their sides of the story, the judge goes back in his office and then makes a decision on the spot in open court—all in a half-hour (minus commercials).

Unfortunately, it doesn't happen that way in the real world. In most instances, courts are costly, inefficient, and slow. In fact, litigants may be in the system for years, especially when the issues involve matters the courts either don't understand or don't handle regularly. Decisions are rarely made on the spot. This means that the very question that must be resolved may not be resolved, or may be delayed too long.

Today, not everyone's needs are best served by using the court system. This is especially true when it comes to unmarried couples. Since you are interested in privacy in your relationship, you should also be interested in a way to resolve your disputes privately. Through alternative dispute resolution techniques, you can try to resolve disputes that otherwise might lead to termination of your relationship. And, if you and your partner do choose to terminate your relationship, you can do so privately, without your personal business being made public. For gay and lesbian couples, especially, the court system is not the best place to resolve disputes.

If you and your partner want to consider alternatives to litigation that can help keep the necessary parts of your relationship intact, you must voluntarily agree to use those alternatives. Alternate dispute resolution techniques are private, faster, and less expensive in time, money, and emotional stress than the court system. Through what is known as "trial by contract," you and your partner can agree on a neutral third party to either mediate your dispute or arbitrate the issues according to relaxed rules and procedures.

Mediation is a non-binding way in which an impartial facilitator who has no coercive powers can begin an exchange and suggest solutions to some of your problems. Mediators can be lawyers, psychologists, or counselors, or someone you both may choose to act as a neutral facilitator. Some states require licensing, while others do not. In any case, if you use mediation, it is unwise to enter into any long-range agreement without using a lawyer to review the matter, because of tax and other consequences.

Arbitration places a third party or a panel of three independent neutrals—lawyers, accountants, or other experts you choose—in a decision-making position. This decision can either be "final and binding" or non-binding, depending on your wishes. Depending on how you prepare your agreement, you can resolve all issues or just one issue through an abbreviated, relaxed, private proceeding.

Because the entire arbitration procedure is governed by the desires of those who utilize it through a contract, you can agree that if the decision of the arbitrator is not challenged by either of you within a specified time—say, 30 days—the decision will be final.

Or there can be "opt out" provisions that allow either of you to take advantage of the court system if you're not happy with the arbitrated result.

If a financial question is presented, you and your partner can even agree to limits through a form of arbitration called "high-low."

Finally, if you decide to use alternative dispute resolution techniques, make sure your lawyer is fully familiar with the type of clauses that will protect you, including how to choose arbitrators, time limits, and rules.

Income Contributions

Frank, a human resources executive, divorced after twenty years of marriage, met Cathy, a divorced real estate agent, who moved in with him. Six months later, Frank found out that Cathy was more than $35,000 behind in child support payments and installment loans. Because he wanted the relationship to work, Frank borrowed the money, put a second mortgage on his house, and paid off Cathy's debts. When the real estate market slowed to a crawl, Frank found himself giving money to Cathy regularly and making Cathy's monthly child support payments. Then, one day, eighteen months after they had met, Cathy was gone...and so was Frank's home.

Divorce, alimony, division of assets, inheritance, and health-care decisions are all creatures of state law written to serve traditional husbands and wives. Since these laws are not applicable to unmarried couples, you have the unique opportunity to design and create your rights and obligations through written contracts, which must be well-thought-out, properly prepared, and tailored to meet your specific needs and intentions.

When it comes to dealing with the financial and property rights of your relationship, as an unmarried couple or "partnership," you have the right to establish and implement arrangements that will allow you to manage your ongoing relationship, to dissolve your relationship if that becomes necessary, and to deal with the after-effects of the death of one or both of you.

Invariably, as with married couples, you and your partner will make both monetary (direct) and non-monetary (indirect) contributions to the economic good of your ongoing relationship, and each of you should receive credit for your contributions. In some instances, for example, one partner may give up a job to move or otherwise help foster the career of the other, or, in addition to working a job, take care of the home. In other relationships, one or both partners will bring inheritance, family gifts, income, and assets into the relationship. And in still others, partners will also be business associates.

You and your partner will pool your money, purchase property, improve property, and incur debt. The result: You and your partner will build a valuable estate that is neither protected by the inheritance laws of your state should one of you die, nor the divorce laws of your state should your relationship terminate for some reason. Because your contributions will build value, you and your partner must decide what goes into the "economic pot," how each of you will be protected in case of death or termination of the relationship, and how to deal with a number of important issues, such as:

- How will gifts and inheritances from families be treated? How will property purchased during the relationship be handled? Who will contribute what amount to the monthly living expense budget? What about gifts from one of you to the other? Who will be responsible for keeping the budget?

- Will you use joint, joint with survivorship, or separate accounts? How will property be titled? Who will be responsible for debts? Who will sign leases, bank notes, car loans, mortgages? How will the contributions of each be tracked? Should there be contracts to make wills?

- How will the economic pie be divided if your relationship ends? What will happen if one of you dies? How will children of a prior marriage be protected? Will either of you will receive support and, if so, how much, for how long, and will the obligation will be secured or funded by life insurance, assets, or by an annuity? Are there tax consequences involved, and how will they be dealt with? How will you resolve your disputes in order to avoid making your personal business a matter of public record?

Because your relationship is not traditional, there are many potential problems that must be recognized and dealt with. For example, what if Jack and Jane acquire a $100,000 home, to which Jack contributed 75 percent of the money. Jane contributed 25 percent of the money but, since she also takes care of the house, Jack and Jane have signed an agreement that provides for a 50–50 division of the property if they terminate their relationship. If, as here, properties are owned in proportions that do not reflect the actual monetary contributions to its price, a very important question arises:

Is this a gift to Jane, who has received a share greater than Jack's direct investment would warrant? Or will Jane be deemed to be receiving income for her services?

What if Jack and Jane pool their incomes and assets? Jack provides 90 percent of the income and therefore contributes 90 percent of the money to the property. Does this mean that Jane is receiving support or other income on which she will be taxed?

If there is to be a support obligation due from one partner to another upon termination of the relationship—and there probably should be if one gives up a career or a job—what should be the amount and for how long should the obligation continue? Since sexual relations are not an enforceable consideration, the agreement must recite appropriate reasons for payment of support, such as housekeeping, secretarial help, decorating services, and so forth. And the tax consequences may be tricky because these payments would most likely be taxable to the recipient and not deductible to the payer.

Tax Issues

The tax considerations affecting unmarried couples are also complex and important. Married couples who are validly wed under state law are able to file joint income tax returns to benefit from favorable rates and deductions, use gift-splitting opportunities to reduce gift taxes, and benefit from the estate or gift tax marital deduction.

Cohabiting couples who are not married, however, cannot take advantage of these tax benefits. Just as importantly, without proper planning, they may find themselves incurring income and gift tax obligations they did not anticipate. For example, partners who shift income or assets to each other, directly or indirectly, may generate income or gift tax liability. And in some instances, employment taxes may be a factor to be considered.

In some coupling arrangements, both partners work and earn either equal or unequal incomes. When both work, one or both also contributes services to the good of the relationship. In other arrangements, one partner may work while the other stays at home.

Unmarried couples usually enter into three basic types of arrangements, which may or may not lead to tax consequences. In some instances, one arrangement may morph into another, so continuing tax and other planning is essential:

Shared Expense Arrangement: If you and your partner form a relationship together solely to divide the cost of a home or apartment and make no exchanges of money or property, there will be no tax consequences.

Service-for-Pay Arrangement: If Jack and Jane have an arrangement by which Jack (the paying partner) pays the expenses of the home and Jane (the service partner) performs agreed services, even though Jack will not be able to deduct the payments, Jane will have income equal to the value of meals and accommodations. And if Jack transfers property to Jane for the services, Jane will have income equal to the fair market value of the property while Jack will be taxed just as if he had sold the property.

True Coupling Arrangement: If Jack and Jane enter into a true "coupling" arrangement, including pooling their income and assets, the tax consequences will vary depending on the financial agreements Jack and Jane make.

If You Separate

When you are writing your plan, you certainly aren't expecting to separate at some point. Nevertheless, you should be aware of issues that may arise if you do separate.

When two individuals live together without the benefit of marriage, share assets and income, acquire assets, and then separate, a whole new set of rules take over. Rather than being governed by a body of statutory and case law and family courts, the relationship is governed by agreements, implied agreements, and intent.

Upon separation, what remedies may be available? First of all, it depends on where you live.

Common-Law Marriage

At present, nine states (Alabama, Colorado, Kansas, Rhode Island, South Carolina, Iowa, Montana, Oklahoma, and Texas), plus the District of Columbia, recognize the doctrine of common-law marriage.

In addition, five states ((Georgia, Idaho, Ohio, Oklahoma, and Pennsylvania) will recognize common-law marriages entered into prior to a specific date set forth in the legislation. Two other states (New Hampshire and Utah) recognize common-law marriage under very limited circumstances.

Common-law marriage can be established when a man and woman intend to be husband and wife and there is mutual, open showing of a marriage relationship. While the ultimate decision is a question of fact for a judge, generally there must be a mutual exchange of promises for the husband-and-wife relationship to be established. The intent is usually proved by evidence of holding themselves out as husband and wife by living together and having community reputation of being husband and wife. Upon proving a common-law marriage, the relationship is governed by the same laws as those governing couples who have ceremonial marriages.

When There Is No Common-Law Marriage

In the majority of states that don't recognize common-law marriage, an unmarried cohabitant may be able to secure equitable relief through the following various equitable remedies:

- **Resulting Trust—Unjust Enrichment:** A resulting trust is an equitable remedy that prevents unjust enrichment of one party at the expense of the other. Generally, unjust enrichment can be found where it would be otherwise unfair for one person to retain the assets accumulated by the parties under a confidential relationship. An unjust enrichment claim is not based on an agreement but on the moral principle that one who receives a benefit must make restitution where retaining the benefit would be unjust.

- **Constructive Trust:** Using its equitable powers, if a court determines that a person is holding either money or property of another that was acquired by unjust, unconscionable, or unlawful means, the court can "impress" a trust in favor of the aggrieved party. The basis for this remedy is where a person holds either funds or property which, in equity and good conscience, should be possessed by the other. A constructive trust may arise when a person holding title has an equitable duty to transfer it to another on the ground that he or she would be unjustly enriched if he were permitted to retain it.

- **"Marriage-Like Relationship":** While the state of Washington doesn't recognize common-law marriage, the Washington courts have applied some community property laws to those unmarried individuals who have cohabitated in a "marriage-like relationship" called a **"meretricious" relationship. The factors** required to establish the meretricious relationship include length of relationship and whether assets were commingled. If so, the court can require an equitable division of assets and debts. In addition, unmarried couples—including same-sex relationships—can sign written agreements that establish their property rights.

Contracts: Express Written Agreements

If the parties signed a written cohabitation agreement, the courts can enforce the agreement based on contract law and the terms of the agreement.

Contracts: Express Oral Agreements

A number of states recognize and enforce express oral contracts for support; however, it is essential that the agreement is not based on meretricious consideration.

Contracts: Implied Agreements

A number of states recognize the existence of contracts implied by the parties. There must be a meeting of the minds as to the essential terms before any agreement will be implied. Where an objection is raised that such contracts are too indefinite and uncertain, the courts nevertheless will imply a test of reasonableness to enforce the contract.

Question: *After 15 years of marriage, I finally came out of the closet and, at age 44, left my wife and two young children. Six months after my divorce, I met a wonderful man who I'd like to live with; he wants the same thing. We don't live in a state where gay marriage is legal, so we simply want to cohabit. The catch is that both of our ex-wives say they will make sure we don't see our children again if we live together. Can they do this?*

Answer: They can certainly try to do so by taking you back to court, which will cost you plenty in attorney fees, discovery, and court costs. In addition, you can expect the polarization of families and friends, grandparents asserting their rights, continuing emotional crises for the children, and years of turmoil.

There are potential financial land mines, too, if you enter into a live-in relationship with your boyfriend and then find out he has a bad financial history and perhaps has gone through bankruptcy. Both homes and relationships have been lost to bail out a new partner, who later bails out of the relationship.

Therefore, we would advise that both you and your partner give and receive full financial disclosure so there will be no surprises later. Ask questions. Let your friend review the last five years of your tax returns, and vice versa. In addition, it might be a good idea to exchange credit reports, review each of your divorce decrees and support orders, and discuss and agree upon who is going to pay for what. Finally, to protect your young children, consider estate planning to protect them by getting new wills and signing durable powers of attorney for financial purposes.

SECTION V:
The End of the Line

14

Burial Disputes and Organ Donation

Family disputes over funeral services and burial arrangements are more common than you might think, especially when, for example, a second spouse is pitted against the children of the first marriage, or when natural children disagree about the arrangements that have been made for cremation or burial.

While few of us would ever expect our burial and estate plan to be the focus of cable television, the burial issues surrounding starlet Anna Nicole Smith and Boston Red Sox great Ted Williams show us what can happen without proper planning. No matter where you live, burial disputes are becoming more commonplace, with no one-size-fits-all solution. (In an apparent attempt to decrease the number of disputes, the state of New York has passed a law giving its citizens the ability to select, in writing, the individual who will be in charge of their remains after they die. New Yorkers can use a form that was developed as part of the law. Or, if they don't sign the form, the state establishes a priority list of individuals to make the decision. See the edited form at the end of this chapter for details.)

In Florida, which has had more than its share of burial litigation, there have been court decisions stating that where there is sufficient proof of a person's intentions, the court should make every effort to carry out that intent when it comes to funeral and burial arrangements. Only where there is no evidence of such a direction by the deceased should the desires of family members be considered.

Which family members would have priority? In Florida, without a clear intention professed, the court would first look to the spouse and, if there is none, to the next of kin to make the burial decision. And in the Sunshine State, even a legally separated spouse has the right to make disposition of the husband's/wife's remains, even if the children object.

On the national level, because of difficulties that have arisen concerning burial decisions for members of our armed forces, the Department of Defense now requires servicemen and women to complete Form 93, wherein decisions about disposition of remains are made.

Put It in Writing

In our view, the best way to make sure your funeral and burial plans are followed is to make them known to your family members in writing—and do so in advance. Moreover, the best way to make sure your desires become reality is to preplan and prepay your arrangements with the cemetery, crematorium, and/or funeral home of your choice while you are able to do so.

Almost all funeral homes will help you preplan your services and burial arrangements, including cremation, while you are alive. In this way, you can avoid potential family squabbles, remove a burden from grieving family members, negotiate your last rights with a clear mind and without being rushed or pressured, and ensure that your instructions are carried out to the letter.

Preplanning includes prepayment to the funeral home for all services that you desire. The funeral home is required by law to keep your funds in a trust account pending your death.

We suggest that your contract with the funeral home be irrevocable. If you have a burial insurance policy, consider either assigning it to the funeral home or making the funeral home the beneficiary. At a minimum, let your personal representative or chosen family members know where these policies can be found. Otherwise, your funeral may be paid for before anyone discovers that your policies even exist.

If you are a veteran, check into benefits that may be available, and make sure that copies of your military papers are available so that the claim can be made in a timely manner.

If you choose to put directions about your last rights in your will, you may want to use a codicil (which is an amendment or addition to your will) that contains only your funeral and burial instructions. You should give your codicil to the funeral home or another person you may appoint to be in charge of your arrangements. But first, check with your lawyer to see if the law in your state protects a personal representative or funeral home that acts according to burial instructions contained in a will or codicil.

And, remember: If you change your mind about your arrangements and don't change your will or codicil, the conflict between the written document and subsequent oral instructions will surely cause a problem. Therefore, any changes you make should be put into writing and delivered to appropriate persons, and the outdated documents should be picked up and destroyed.

Donating Organs or Your Body

If you wish to be an organ donor or to leave your body to a medical school, there are laws you must follow. Moreover, it's a good idea to let your family know about your wishes while you are still alive.

Like giving blood, the organ donation system in the United States is voluntary. All states and the District of Columbia have passed the Uniform Anatomical Gift Act (U.A.G.A.) in either its 1968 or 1987 form. This law basically provides that if you are 18 years of age or older and have the capacity to make the decision, you can make a gift, effective at death, of all or part of your body for permitted purposes. According to federal law, the sale of organs is prohibited. State laws also include a list of people, including certain relatives, court-appointed guardians, and other persons who have the right to dispose of your body, to make donations after or immediately prior to death. In some states, if authorized by the terms of a durable power of attorney, your agent is allowed to make the donation.

While an anatomical gift can be made by your will, this is probably not a good idea because your will might not be available at or near the time of death. The better practice is to include the gift in your health care power of attorney, on a card you carry with you, or, as is done in many states, by having your choice placed on your driver's license. In all states, the gifting document must be signed by you, and some states require witnesses.

State laws include a list of acceptable organ recipients, which include medical schools, hospitals, doctors, or named individuals. After death and the removal of the organs, the remainder of the body is turned over to the person having the responsibility of ensuring burial, cremation, or other arrangements—generally, the surviving spouse or next of kin. If you wish to donate your body to a medical school for research, you should make these arrangements directly with the school before death.

So long as you have capacity, you may change or revoke the gift at any time before death. Because death is such a traumatic time for families, in order to assure that your wishes are carried out, you should make your intention to donate your organs or body known to your family. If you don't do so, your family will be in a position to "veto" your donation decision. Like other aspects of the planning process, full disclosure to family members avoids surprise and helps avert unpleasantness at a time when you can not express your desires.

In general, assuming good heath, the upper age limitations for donors are as follows: kidney, ages 70-75; heart, ages 55-60; lung, age 70; heart-lung, age 55; liver, age 70; cornea, no age limit; skin, age 75; bone, age 55; and heart valves, age 55. For more information, you may wish to contact the American Red Cross, the Living Bank, or the United Network for Organ Sharing (UNOS).

Burial Directives

The United States Department of Defense issued an order that all service personnel name an agent to take custody of remains. In New York, Public Health Law 4201 is not mandatory, and there may be no such laws in other states; however, those of us who want to control where and how our remains are disposed of should put our wishes in writing.

Here is an edited version of the New York statutory example:

**FORMAT BASED ON NEW YORK STATUTORY LAW—
NOT TO BE USED WITHOUT ADVICE OF AN ATTORNEY.
FOR INFORMATIONAL PURPOSES ONLY.**

STATE OF _____   )

)   TRUST AGREEMENT

COUNTY OF _____   )

ARTICLE I—APPOINTMENT OF AGENT TO CONTROL DISPOSITION OF REMAINS

Being of sound mind, willfully and voluntarily make known my desire that, upon my death the disposition of my remains shall be controlled by _____. With respect to that subject only, I hereby appoint such person as my trustee and agent with respect to the disposition of my remains.

ARTICLE II—SPECIAL DIRECTIONS

Set forth below are my special directions limiting the power granted to my trustee and agent as well as any instructions or wishes desired to be followed in the disposition of my remains:

_____

_____

_____

Indicate below if you have entered into a pre-funded pre-need, funeral agreement subject to the laws of this state concerning funerals and pre-need services.

☐ No, I have not entered into a pre-funded pre-need agreement

☐ Yes, I have entered into a pre-funded pre-need agreement with

_____

_____

(Name of funeral firm with which you entered into a pre-funded, pre-need funeral agreement to provide merchandise and/or services.)

ARTICLE III—TRUSTEE/AGENT APPOINTED

Trustee/Agent's Name:_____

Trustee/Agent's Address: _____

Telephone: Home: _____ Work: _____
Mobile: _____

ARTICLE IV—SUCCESSOR TRUSTEES/AGENTS

If my trustee/agent dies, resigns, or is unable to act, I hereby appoint the following persons (each to act alone and successively, in the order named) to serve as my trustee/agent to control the disposition of my remains as authorized by this document:

a. First Successor: _____

Successor's Address: _____

Telephone: Home: _____ Work: _____
Mobile: _____

b. Second Successor: _____

Successor's Address: _____

Telephone: Home: _____ Work: _____
Mobile: _____

ARTICLE V—DURATION

The appointment of my Trustee/Agent becomes effective upon my death.

ARTICLE VI—PRIOR APPOINTMENT REVOKED

I hereby revoke any prior appointment of any person to control the disposition of my remains. Signed this _____ day of _____.

_____

Signature of person making appointment

Statement by witness (must be 18 or older): I declare that the person who signed this document is personally known to me and appears to be of sound mind and acting of his or her free will. He or she signed (or asked another to sign for him or her) this document in my presence.

_____

Witness #1 Signature

_____

(Printed Name of **Witness #1**)

_____

Address

_____

Witness #2 Signature

_____

(Printed Name of **Witness #2**)

_____

Address

ARTICLE VII—ACCEPTANCE AND ASSUMPTION BY TRUSTEE/AGENT

I have no reason to believe that there have been any revocations of this appointment to control disposition of remains. I hereby accept this appointment. Signed this _____ day of _____.

_____

(Signature of Trustee/Agent)

ARTICLE VIII—PRIORITY, IF FORM NOT USED

The Trustee/Agent appointed here—and all successors should my first appointment fail or refuse to act—have the primary and absolute right to control disposition of my remains. If my Trustee/Agent and alternate Trustees/Agents do not act, then the following priority is established to carry out the terms of this trust: my spouse, my domestic partner, my children over the age of 18 in order of birth, either of my parents, or my siblings over the age of 18 in order of birth.

QUESTION: *I am a widower, 76, with no children and few relatives. My wife died six years ago and, according to her wishes, her body was cremated and her ashes were buried in our backyard. My health is not terrible, but not the best either. I had planned to also be cremated, but I have no close relative who will dispose of my ashes, etc.*

I began looking into donating my body to our local medical school, but the forms they sent me were one-sided and give the school so many outs to not take my body that I worry what will happen if my remains are not accepted and I have no alternate plans. I know this sounds nutty, but I have been losing sleep thinking about what will happen to my remains when I die. I am leaving everything my wife and I acquired to our favorite charities. Can you give me some ideas, and do I need a lawyer to assist me in this endeavor?

ANSWER: Unlike an organ donation where specific tissue is removed from the body of a person who died recently or from a living donor for the purpose of transplantation into other persons, the anatomical gift you are speaking of involves leaving your body to be dissected by medical students or for other educational or research purposes.

In 1968, the Uniform Anatomical Gift Act was enacted in order to create a standardized approach to comprehensive and standardized laws regarding organ and tissue donations. Today, all 50 states and the District of Columbia follow this act in one form or another (some with slight variations).

Unlike organ donations that can be opted for on your driver's license, cadaver donations require more documentation. That's why, generally speaking, you should rely on the documents provided by the medical school of your choice.

Without these written documents in place, there will be problems because you will not have an advocate available after you die to enforce your wishes.

Although some health conditions may render a cadaver unsuitable for donation (like, for example, infectious diseases, severe obesity, autopsy, or decomposition), the bodies of those with other medical conditions (such as dementia, Parkinson's, etc.) may be very valuable for research into those conditions.

While all medical schools in the United States depend on donors to teach anatomy, there are conditions for accepting cadavers. For example, some medical schools will pay for or contribute to the expense of the funeral home delivering the body to the school. Generally, the remains will be either cremated or buried after the course is completed, but some schools require the donor to make an up-front payment to cover the cost of final disposal. And all of the forms we have reviewed contain the clear warning to the donor that because acceptance of the body is not guaranteed, alternate disposal arrangements should be made.

TAKING THE NEXTSTEP: If you choose to make an anatomical gift of your body to a medical school for research or education, make sure to get your papers together as early as possible. We suggest that if you have the time and the distance is not too great, you should make an appointment with the proper persons at the medical school and discuss your concerns. And since there is no guarantee that your body will ultimately be accepted, we recommend that you create a contingency plan whereby your personal representative ensures that your remains are either cremated or buried.

15

Planning for Pets

Each year, billions of dollars are spent on pet care. In fact, according to some studies, pets live in more than 60 percent of American households. Little wonder, then, that more and more Americans proactively seek methods of protecting their dogs, cats, birds, and other pets should they (their humans) become incapacitated or die.

Today, especially among the elderly and disabled who either have no family or are not particularly close to their family, pets have become the most trusted source of companionship, trust, and affection. For this reason, many seniors want to leave funds at death (or in the event of incapacitation) to ensure that their pets will be cared for. (It is estimated that about 25 percent of pet owners provide for pet care in their wills, even though pets can't inherit property directly.)

The late real estate/hotel magnate Leona Helmsley is a case in point. While the size of the multimillion dollar trust she set up for her dog is certainly the exception, pet trusts are now available, via legislation, in many states. In fact, the Uniform Trust Act of 2000, adopted in a number of states, allows trusts for pet care and even permits judges to appoint guardians to enforce the terms of the trust. The basic requirements are that the animal be alive during the life of the creator of the trust; the court can appoint a person to enforce the trust; a person interested in the welfare of the animal can request that the court remove the caregiver; and, remaining assets go to the creator's chosen beneficiary or heirs at the death of the pet.

Still, the question that haunts many seniors is: How can I make sure, if I die or become disabled, that my pets are taken care of? Some elders mistakenly believe that family members and/or friends will take care of their pets, even though the seniors haven't put anything in writing. The devotion of substitute caregivers often is not there, and it takes time and money to properly care for a pet.

Moreover, even if the right person is found, other questions arise. Who will keep the pet and where? Will the pet be difficult to keep after the senior dies because of behavioral problems? Who will make sure the pet is fed, given medical attention, and kept groomed? How much money will it take to maintain the pet until it dies, and if there is any money left, who or what will receive it?

Some seniors decide to put their wishes for their pets into their wills. But because your will could be held up in probate for a time, or could be subject to challenges, we believe the safest method for protecting your pets is to create a trust now, and either fund it now (if you have the funds) or figure out how to fund it based on the occurrence of an event, such as your incapacity or death.

By creating a stand-alone trust now, you can avoid probate, protect your pet if you become disabled, and make sure your pet has immediate care.

Setting Up a Trust for Your Pet

First of all, never leave important decisions like setting up a trust for your animal to verbal arrangements and promises. To make sure that your wishes are carried out, use formal documents. The last thing you want is to give or leave funds to friends or family members who, while promising to care for your pets, take the money and do nothing. Put everything in writing and engage a lawyer who understands what you need, and who also understands the legalities of setting up the trust.

How much you should leave in your trust, and the source of funds for the trust, are two other questions you must consider. Determining factors can include the number of pets; your annual budget for your pets; the ages, health condition, and the estimated life of your pets (for example, it will take more money to care for a young cat than for an older parakeet). And, if you have animals that are susceptible to hip dysplasia or other ailments, or in the future might be afflicted with diabetes or cancer, you should decide just how far your trustee should be required to go with treatment. Similarly, you should be specific about the cost of burial or cremation, and possibly pay this expense in advance to avoid future price increases.

If you have funding issues, you may want to make your trustee the beneficiary of an insurance policy on your life.

As part of the process of setting up a trust for your pet, we suggest that you consider the following:

- Instead of providing that the trustee receive the remaining money after the demise of the pet, the trustee instead be paid a fee for so long as the pet lives. This is an economic incentive to care for the pet in the best way possible and for as long as possible.

- The language of the trust gives the trustee the right to euthanize the pet if a trusted veterinarian decides the pet is suffering.

- Burial instructions be included.

In addition, to be on the safe side, in some instances you may want to consider having two individuals involved in your trust—a pet guardian to handle the day-to-day care and a trustee to handle the funds.

At the pet's death, we suggest choosing a beneficiary of the remaining funds who is not involved in the care of the pet, and also setting up a contingent bequest—that is, a bonus to the caregiver based on the type of care provided for the pet and the pet's longevity.

Another Option

Another possible solution is for pet owners to give money to animal-related charities in exchange for those entities providing for a pet's care during its life. There are charities available for horses and other pets. For this reason, some planners suggest that a sum be left to a charity on the condition that it cares for the pet after the owner's death or disability.

Other Things to Do for Your Pet

- If your pet has health problems, include directives in your trust and/or power of attorney about which veterinarian to use, special diets, medications, and related instructions. You should also contact your veterinarian in advance and let him or her know who will be providing for your pet should you be unable to do so.

- Always inform your agent or your trustee for pet purposes when you go to the hospital or will not be home so that your pet will be fed and cared for on a daily basis. Too many times, when individuals have emergency treatment or hospitalization, pets are left at home without care.

- If you have more than one pet, address legitimate questions of whether the animals should be split up or kept together and, in either case, who would be the best caregiver. If your pets have bonded and need to be kept together, it may be difficult finding an appropriate caregiver. In choosing a caregiver for your pet, always look to those who have properly cared for pets in the past. And, always name at least two alternates.

- The selection process should include conversations with prospective caregivers about what you expect in order to make sure the caregiver understands exactly how you want your pet(s) cared for.

- If you can't think of a possible caregiver for your pet, you could allow your agent or personal representative to make the choice, but we don't think this is an especially good idea. Talk to your veterinarian and find out if he or she knows people or non-institutional care-giving associations that can help.

- If you become incapacitated, ask about temporary housing for your pet until a permanent situation can be determined.

- Make sure your document identifies your pet not only by name, but also by breed, color, and even tattoos so there is no question about identification. You should also consider including information about diet, health issues, behavioral quirks, and veterinary documentation.

QUESTION: *My husband and I, each age 81, are not in good health. We have no children, but we do have a dog that means the world to us. How can we make sure that Gretchen, our 5-year-old terrier, is taken care of when we die?*

ANSWER: You are right to think about this issue now. It's not a given that family members and/or friends will take care of Gretchen after you're gone because of the time and money issues involved.

You could put your wishes for Gretchen in your wills, but that's not necessarily the best choice, because your will could be held up in probate for a time or be subject to challenges. In our view, the best method of protecting your dog is to create a trust, and either fund it now (if you can), or decide how to fund it when you die or become incapacitated. Be creating a stand-alone trust now, you can avoid probate, protect Gretchen if you become disabled, and make sure she has immediate care.

You need formal documents to set up a trust for your pets. Put everything in writing and hire a lawyer who understands what you want and also understands the legalities of setting up this type of trust. How much you should leave in your trust depends on Gretchen's health and life expectancy. You could discuss this with your veterinarian. And, you should be specific about the cost of burial or cremation for your dog, and perhaps pay this expense in advance to avoid future price increases.

If you have funding issues, consider making your trustee the beneficiary of an insurance policy on your life. The trustee would then use this money to care for your dog for the rest of her life.

Another possible solution is for you and your husband to give money to animal-related charities in exchange for those entities providing for a pet's care during its life. We have heard from readers that this works nicely.

Epilogue

So, where do we go from here?

With octogenarians the country's fastest-growing population segment, and considering the declining economic status of the United States (and the world), appropriate planning requires that we look at the legal, emotional, ethical, medical, and economic issues involved in end-of-life planning—*before* we become incapacitated.

In 1991, the federal Patient Self Determination Act (PSDA) became law, requiring health-care providers to educate patients and consumers about advance health care directives—that is, living wills and health care powers of attorney. This law is the reason that when you and I go into the hospital, we are asked if we have a living will.

One of the driving forces behind PSDA was end-of-life health-care costs, which were extremely costly to the Medicare program. In the early 1990s, according to government statistics, a significant portion of all health-care expenses were incurred during the last year of life, most during the last two months.

At the same time, the American Medical Association has estimated that although more than 70 percent of Americans will face at least one end-of-life decision during their lifetimes, fewer than

15 percent have signed advance directives. As outlined in an article in the *Archives of Internal Medicine*, the end-of-life costs for patients without advance directives are approximately three times higher than for patients who had prepared these documents. Why? Because the vast majority of those who sign advance directives choose less life-sustaining intervention at the end of life. (A 1990 Gallup Poll found that 84 percent of Americans would choose to withhold medical treatment if they were on life-sustaining equipment with no chance of recovery.)

So, where does this leave us today? It leaves us with law in this area being made on a state-by-state basis.

The Oregon Death with Dignity Act (Or. Rev. Stat.§§ 127.800-.995 [2005]) allows Oregon residents who are mentally competent and have less than six months to live (as confirmed by two physicians) to secure a prescription for medication they can self-administer to bring on a peaceful death—on the patient's terms and schedule. As part of the strict procedures required by the law, the patient must be informed about palliative care options, such as hospice. If a provider of health care objects to participation for religious or moral reasons, he or she can't be required to become involved.

In November 2008, Washington state voters approved the Washington Death with Dignity Act by a 59 to 41 percent vote. This law has basically the same protections as the Oregon law. And, Montana's Supreme Court has determined that the state's constitutional rights of privacy and dignity include the right to make choices in dying that are based upon one's personal autonomy and decisions.

The goal of all these laws, of course, is to establish methods to exercise choice and also to reduce costs without sacrificing quality of life or palliative (pain management) care. Clearly, Americans believe these decisions should not be made by government, but instead by themselves and their families, with the assistance of physicians.

But this will not happen magically. You will be able to control your destiny during the second half of life *only* if you act now to take the necessary next steps. This means putting together the right professional team to devise the right plan for you, and then signing appropriate legal documents to ensure that your wishes will be carried out and your family will be protected.

If you haven't done so already, it's past time to take those next steps.

Glossary

Here are some terms with which you should familiarize yourself:

Advance Directive:
One's expression of preferences about medical treatment (or non treatment) made before mental incapacity. A generic term that includes such documents as living wills, health care powers of attorney, and medical directives. **No advance directive can be used unless or until the patient is unable to make his or her own health-care decisions.**

Artificially-provided, Nutrition/Hydration:

Called "ANH", refers to any of several methods for providing nutrition and hydration to patients who are unable (or unwilling) to take in food and fluids by mouth. Often called "tube feeding," and includes giving nutrition and fluids through a tube in the veins, nose, or stomach.

Best Interests: Absent an advance directive, states have enacted health care consent statutes by which substitute decision makers are enabled to make health-care decisions for incapacitated persons. Because of the wording of many of these statutes, there are disagreements among potential decision makers, which result in court proceedings. There are issues about whether this type of decision maker can make end-of-life decisions. This is one of the standards by which third persons can make health-care decisions for mentally incapacitated patients based on what the decision maker believes to be "best" for the patient.

Conservator:

A person appointed by a court to manage the assets of an incapacitated ward in a legal proceeding.

Durable Health Care Power of Attorney:

Document by which a person appoints an agent to make a broad range of health-care decisions that are not limited to end-of-life situations. See Living Will below.

Guardian:

A person appointed by a court to manage the health care, placement, and related duties of an incapacitated ward in a legal proceeding.

Guardian ad Litem:

A person appointed by a court to protect the interests of an incapacitated person in a legal proceeding.

Heroic Measures:

A non-specific, non-medical term by which individuals intend to define the various types of artificial life support, tube feeding, and other end-of-life medical interventions.

Incompetent/Incapacitated:

Persons are incompetent or incapacitated to make medical decisions when they are either 1) no longer able to understand information about their medical condition and its implications, or 2) are able to understand but unable to communicate decisions. A patient's ability to understand other unrelated concepts is not relevant.

246

Living Will:

A type of advance directive signed while a person is able to make health care decisions expressing preferences for only **end-of-life medical treatment (or non-treatment)** in the event of a terminal illness or injury. The law of each state defines the scope of application.

Persistent Vegetative State:

Sometimes referred to as "permanent unconsciousness," this term means that although there may be motor reflexes, brain function is permanently lost.

Power of Attorney:

A type of advance directive appointing an agent to make a broad range of health-care decisions that are **not limited to end-of-life situations, but can include a broad range of treatment**. "Durable" means that the document remains in effect after the individual who signs it is unable to express his/her decisions.

State Interests:

Right-to-die decisions typically weigh the patient's right to refuse life-sustaining treatment against four state interests: 1) the preservation of life, 2) the prevention of suicide (usually not implicated because death which occurs after the removal of life support is due to natural causes, not intended or set in motion by the patient), 3) protection of innocent third parties, and 4) safeguarding the integrity of the medical profession.

Substituted Judgment:

Absent an advance directive where an individual does not specifically state his/her end-of-life wishes, this is another standard by which third persons may make health-care decisions for incapacitated patients. Here, the decision maker evaluates the patient's past statements, attitudes, and beliefs about end-of-life issues. The decision maker stands in the patient's shoes and makes the decision he or she believes the patient would have made under those circumstances, thus substituting his/her judgment for the patient's.

Terminal Illness, Terminal Condition:

Although the definition of "terminal" varies from state to state, the focus is generally on life expectancy and/or the possibility of a return to cognitive life.

Web Resources

Next Steps Websites

Full of helpful information and services, be sure to visit the authors' websites:

www.nextsteps.net

www.flyingsolo.com

www.lifemanagement.com

Professional Services

www.caremanager.org
The National Association of Professional Geriatric Care Managers.

www.naela.org
The National Association of Elder Law Attorneys.

www.aaml.org
The American Academy of Matrimonial Lawyers.

www.adviserinfo.sec.gov/IAPD/Content/Search/iapd_OrgSearch.
aspx
To check investment advisors.

www.finra.org/Investors/ToolsCalculators/BrokerCheck/index.htm
To check brokers.

Medical Information

www.webmd.com/alzheimers/guide/alzheimers-dementia
Information on Alzheimer's disease and dementia.

www.alz.org
The Alzheimer's Association.

www.mda.org
The Muscular Dystrophy Association.

www.nationalmssociety.org
The National Muscular Sclerosis Society.

www.stroke.org
The National Stroke Association.

www.nlm.nih.gov/medlineplus/rehabilitation.html
Rehabilitation information and resources.

physicaltherapy.about.com
Information on physical therapy.

www.aota.org/Consumers.aspx
The American Occupational Therapy Association.

en.wikipedia.org/wiki/Speech_and_language_pathology
Information on speech and language pathology and therapy.

www.aphasia.org
The National Aphasia Organization.

www.asha.org/public/speech/disorders/Aphasia.htm
American Speech-Language-Hearing Association.

en.wikipedia.org/wiki/Aphasia
Information on aphasia and dysphasia.

Non-medical Caregivers

www.visitingangels.com
In-home care services.

www.homeinstead.com/home.aspx
In-home care services.

www.stepfamilies-international.org
Information, support, advice, and tangible goods for families.

Helpful Resources

www.aarp.org
The AARP.

Government Websites

www.irs.gov/publications/index.html
List of online IRS publications.

www.ssa.gov
Social Security.

www.medicare.gov
Medicare.

www.cms.hhs.gov
Medicaid.

64.82.65.67/medicaid/states.html
Medicaid Programs by state.

Index

JAN WARNER received his A.B. and J.D. degrees from the University of South Carolina and earned a Master of Legal Letters (L.L.M.) in Taxation from the Emory University School of Law in Atlanta, Georgia. He is the founding partner and share-holder of ElderLaw Services of South Carolina, P.A./Warner Payne & Black, L.L.P., a law firm that limits its practice to matters affecting the family and the elderly including estate and long-term care planning, planning for incapacity, Medicaid qualification, and litigation in South Carolina courts. He has been a frequent lecturer at both legal education and public information programs sponsored by The American Bar Association, various state and metropolitan bar associations, and other professional organizations and associations. His articles have been published in national and state legal publications.

Warner conceived and for 20 years has co-authored **Flying Solo**®, a weekly newspaper column about divorce. He also conceived and for 11 years has co-authored **NextSteps**®, a weekly newspaper column about matters affecting the elderly, both syndicated by United Media (United Features Syndicate). Both columns have established Internet presences (**www.flyingsolo.com** and **www.nextsteps.net**). He also has hosted **NextSteps**® **Senior Talk**™, a talk radio program regarding issues affecting the elderly and disabled.

He founded **Life Management**® in 1988 and has produced series of audiotapes, videotapes, and print materials concerning divorce and separation, death of a spouse, and issues affecting the elderly. By virtue of a license granted by the American Bar Association, Life Management® has produced audiotapes in a series for the Family Law Section.

His **Make Your Wishes Known**® programs were partially funded by The Duke Endowment and were produced in association with The South Carolina Hospital Association and Mary Black Foundation. This series of audiotapes, video-tapes, and print materials which deal with the health care decision-making process is hosted by **Spencer Christian**, formerly of ABC's *Good Morning America*, and has been endorsed by hospital associations throughout the United States. These programs have been designated as a national resource by the Department of Health and Human Services and have been positively reviewed by *The Annenberg Washington White Paper*.

He and his programs have been featured on radio and television throughout the United States and written about in the press and legal publications—including *Kiplinger's*, *ABA Journal*, *National Law Journal*, *USA Weekend*, *People*, *Detroit Free Press*, *Entertainment Weekly*, *USA Today*, *NY Post*, *The Wall Street Journal*, *LA Times*, *Dallas Morning News*, *Plain Dealer* (Cleveland), and *Washington Post*. He has been quoted in *Kiplinger's*, *Modern Maturity*, and the *Wall Street Journal*, among others.

JAN COLLINS began coauthoring **Flying Solo**® in 1989 and **NextSteps**™ in 1998. She has more than 40 years of experience as a journalist, writer, and editor. She has worked as a reporter for newspapers in Michigan, North Carolina, and South Carolina, and has been an editor and writer at the Moore School of Business, University of South Carolina, since 1983.

Ms. Collins is also a special correspondent for *The (London) Economist*. She has published hundreds of articles and contributed chapters to three books, and has won numerous awards for her writing and editing.

She was granted a Nieman Fellowship at Harvard University and a Congressional Fellowship in Washington, D.C. Ms. Collins is a member of the American Society of Journalists and Authors (ASJA).

Jan Collins holds a bachelor's degree from Georgetown University and a master's degree from the University of Michigan. Visit her website at www.jan-collins.com.

Visit the authors' information websites: **www.nextsteps.net**, **www.flyingsolo.com**, and **www.lifemanagement.com**.